The Book of Occasional Services

The Church Hymnal Corporation
800 Second Avenue, New York, N.Y. 10017

Table of Contents

Preface

This book has been prepared by the Standing Liturgical Commission in response to a directive from the General Convention of 1976 to provide a new edition of *The Book of Offices* to replace the third edition of 1960. There had been two previous editions in 1940 and 1949. Some of the material included in those books proved of such value (for example, the form for the adoption of children) that it was included in The Book of Common Prayer. Services from *The Book of Offices* for which there continues to be a need have been retained and revised. In addition, other services and texts have been included in this new edition in response to expressions of need.

All of the material in this book is optional. None of it is required, and no congregation is likely to make use of all of it.

Many valuable suggestions have come from members of the clergy and the laity of the Church. All suggestions have been carefully weighed. Forms in local use which were submitted to the Commission were examined, and many elements from them have been incorporated. Those services which have ancient roots have been studied in their historic forms. Many of the texts and ceremonies included in this book have a very long history indeed (for example, the rites of the catechumenate). Others have been designed to meet needs which have arisen only in recent years (for example, the festivals of lessons and music).

The name of the book has been changed to *The Book of Occasional Services*, in order to express more specifically the contents of the book, and to avoid confusion with that section of the Prayer Book called the Daily Office.

The various parts of this book were drafted by sub-committees and then submitted to the Committee on the Book of Occasional Services for approval and revision, before being considered by the Standing Liturgical Commission. Once approved by the Commission, many of the forms were distributed to diocesan liturgical commissions for their reactions and comments. This process resulted in a number of helpful emendations. A committee of the Standing Commission on Church Music has also examined the material and made valuable suggestions.

The Commission desires to place on record its appreciation to the Rev. Dr. Marion J. Hatchett, Chairman of the committee which reviewed the work of various sub-committees responsible for sections of this book. To the many correspondents who made suggestions and offered criticisms, all of which were greatly valued, even when they were not always followed, the Commission wishes to express its deep gratitude. Those who worked on this book are too many to be listed. Their sense of having contributed to the enrichment of the Church's worship is their own best reward. The Commission can only state that without them this book would not have been possible.

The Standing Liturgical Commission
Feast of the Annunciation, 1979

The Church Year

Anthems at
the Candle Lighting

*The anthems (Lucernaria) which follow are intended for optional use at
the Order of Worship for the Evening as provided for in the second
rubric on page 112 of the Prayer Book. They are arranged for
responsorial performance by a cantor or reader and the congregation.
All repeat the complete refrain after the cantor, and the second half of
the refrain after the verse which follows. The Lucernarium then
concludes with the first half of the Gloria Patri, followed by the
complete refrain.*

*The Versicle which follows is sung or said by the officiant or by a cantor.
Any of the Versicles may be used with any of the Lucernaria.*

*When these anthems are used, it is appropriate to omit the Short Lesson
which precedes the Prayer for Light.*

1

You, O Lord, are my lamp; *
my God, you make my darkness bright.
*You, O Lord, are my lamp;
my God, you make my darkness bright.*
You have been my helper:
My God, you make my darkness bright.
Glory to the Father, and to the Son, and to the Holy Spirit.
*You, O Lord, are my lamp;
my God, you make my darkness bright.*

V. Let my prayer be set forth, O Lord:
R. As incense in your sight.

2

The Lord is my light * and my salvation.
The Lord is my light and my salvation.
The Lord is the strength of my life:
And my salvation.
Glory to the Father, and to the Son, and to the Holy Spirit.
The Lord is my light and my salvation.

V. I will bless the Lord at all times:
R. His praise shall ever be in my mouth.

3

With you, O Lord, is the well of life, *
and in your light we see light.
With you, O Lord, is the well of life,
and in your light we see light.
Your love, O Lord, reaches to the heavens,
and your faithfulness to the clouds:
And in your light we see light.
Glory to the Father, and to the Son, and to the Holy Spirit.
With you, O Lord, is the well of life,
and in your light we see light.

V. Abide with us, O Lord:
R. For it is toward evening.

4

From the rising of the sun to its going down, *
let the Name of the Lord be praised.
From the rising of the sun to its going down,
let the Name of the Lord be praised.
From this time forth for evermore:

Let the Name of the Lord be praised.
Glory to the Father, and to the Son, and to the Holy Spirit.
From the rising of the sun to its going down,
let the Name of the Lord be praised.

V.   The sun knows the time of its setting:
R.   You make darkness that it may be night.

The anthems which follow may be used at the times indicated.
Alternatively, one of the general Lucernaria given above may be used,
followed by the appropriate seasonal Versicle.

Advent

Come and save us, *   O Lord God of hosts.
Come and save us, O Lord God of hosts.
Show the light of your countenance, and we shall be saved:
O Lord God of hosts.
Glory to the Father, and to the Son, and to the Holy Spirit.
Come and save us, O Lord God of hosts.

V.   Show us your mercy, O Lord:
R.   And grant us your salvation.

Christmas

The Word was made flesh, *   alleluia, alleluia.
The Word was made flesh, alleluia, alleluia.
And dwelt among us:
Alleluia, alleluia.
Glory to the Father, and to the Son, and to the Holy Spirit.
The Word was made flesh, alleluia, alleluia.

V.   Blessed is he who comes in the name of the Lord, alleluia:
R.   God is the Lord; he has shined upon us, alleluia.

Epiphany   *(through the following Saturday evening)*

All nations shall be blessed in him, * and do him service.
All nations shall be blessed in him, and do him service.
All kings shall bow down before him:
And do him service.
Glory to the Father, and to the Son, and to the Holy Spirit.
All nations shall be blessed in him, and do him service.

V.   The kings of Tarshish and the isles shall pay tribute:
R.   The kings of Arabia and Saba shall offer gifts.

Lent

I make my prayer to you, O God; * be merciful to me.
I make my prayer to you, O God; be merciful to me.
Heal my soul, for I have sinned against you:
Be merciful to me.
Glory to the Father, and to the Son, and to the Holy Spirit.
I make my prayer to you, O God, be merciful to me.

V.   Create in me a clean heart, O God:
R.   And renew a right spirit within me.

Easter   *(until Ascension Day)*

The Lord is risen from the tomb, * alleluia, alleluia.
The Lord is risen from the tomb, alleluia, alleluia.
Who for our sake hung upon the Tree:
Alleluia, alleluia.
Glory to the Father, and to the Son, and to the Holy Spirit.
The Lord is risen from the tomb, alleluia, alleluia.

V.   The disciples were glad, alleluia:
R.   When they saw the risen Lord, alleluia.

Ascension   *(until the Day of Pentecost)*

God has gone up with a shout, *   alleluia, alleluia.
God has gone up with a shout, alleluia, alleluia.
The Lord with the sound of the ram's-horn:
Alleluia, alleluia.
Glory to the Father, and to the Son, and to the Holy Spirit.
God has gone up with a shout, alleluia, alleluia.

V.   When Christ ascended up on high, alleluia:
R.   He led captivity captive, alleluia.

The Day of Pentecost

The Spirit of the Lord now fills the whole world, *
alleluia, alleluia.
*The Spirit of the Lord now fills the whole world,
alleluia, alleluia.*
The Spirit who searches even the depths of God:
Alleluia, alleluia.
Glory to the Father, and to the Son, and to the Holy Spirit.
*The Spirit of the Lord now fills the whole world,
alleluia, alleluia.*

V.   The apostles spoke in other tongues, alleluia:
R.   The wonderful works of God, alleluia.

Trinity Sunday

Glory to you, O Lord, *   in the high vault of heaven.
Glory to you, O Lord, in the high vault of heaven.
You are worthy of glory and praise for ever:
In the high vault of heaven.
Glory to the Father, and to the Son, and to the Holy Spirit.
Glory to you, O Lord, in the high vault of heaven.

V.   Let us glorify the Lord: Father, Son, and Holy Spirit:
R.   Praise him and highly exalt him for ever.

Feasts of the Incarnation

The Word was made flesh, * and dwelt among us.
The Word was made flesh, and dwelt among us.
He was with God in the beginning:
And dwelt among us.
Glory to the Father, and to the Son, and to the Holy Spirit.
The Word was made flesh, and dwelt among us.

V.   Blessed is he who comes in the name of the Lord:
R.   God is the Lord; he has shined upon us.

On Feasts of the Incarnation in Easter Season, the anthem and versicle for Christmas Season are used.

All Saints' Day and other Major Saints' Days

Let the righteous rejoice * in the presence of God.
Let the righteous rejoice in the presence of God.
Let them be merry and joyful:
In the presence of God.
Glory to the Father, and to the Son, and to the Holy Spirit.
Let the righteous rejoice in the presence of God.

V.   Their sound has gone out into all lands:
R.   And their message to the ends of the world.

Major Saints' Days in Easter Season

Their sound has gone out into all lands, * alleluia, alleluia.
Their sound has gone out into all lands, alleluia, alleluia.
And their message to the ends of the world:
Alleluia, alleluia.

Glory to the Father, and to the Son, and to the Holy Spirit.
Their sound has gone out into all lands, alleluia, alleluia.

V. Let the righteous rejoice, alleluia:
R. In the presence of God, alleluia.

Transfiguration and Holy Cross Day

When I am lifted up, * I will draw the whole world to myself.
When I am lifted up, I will draw the whole world to myself.
I am the light of the world:
I will draw the whole world to myself.
Glory to the Father, and to the Son, and to the Holy Spirit.
When I am lifted up, I will draw the whole world to myself.

V. All the ends of the earth shall see:
R. The salvation of our God.

*If, instead of one of the preceding anthems, it is desired to sing a
complete psalm at this point in the service, one of the evening psalms
listed on page 143 of the Prayer Book may be used.*

Anthems at the Breaking of Bread

One or more anthems may be used at the Breaking of the Bread.

The anthems (Confractoria) which follow are of varying length, and should be chosen on the basis of the time required for the Bread-breaking (whether of a whole loaf or of a number of large wafers), and for their seasonal appropriateness.

It should be noted that the rubrics of the Prayer Book require that the initial breaking of the Bread take place in silence. A distinct period of silence then follows (the celebrant having replaced the Bread on the paten). The singing of the Confractorium is then begun, during which the celebrant and other priests break the Bread for distribution. In the absence of a sufficient number of priests, deacons may assist in the Bread-breaking. The pouring of consecrated Wine into any additional chalices should also take place during this anthem, and before the Invitation "The Gifts of God . . ." and the celebrant's communion.

1

Christ our Passover is sacrificed for us;
Therefore let us keep the feast.

2

The bread which we break is a sharing in the Body of Christ.
We being many are one bread, one body,
for we all share in the one bread.

3

O Lamb of God, that takest away the sins of the world,
have mercy upon us.
O Lamb of God, that takest away the sins of the world,
have mercy upon us.
O Lamb of God, that takest away the sins of the world,
grant us thy peace.

4

Lamb of God, you take away the sins of the world:
have mercy on us.
Lamb of God, you take away the sins of the world:
have mercy on us.
Lamb of God, you take away the sins of the world:
grant us peace.

5

My flesh is food indeed, and my blood is drink indeed,
says the Lord.
My flesh is food indeed, and my blood is drink indeed,
says the Lord.
Those who eat my flesh and drink my blood dwell in me
and I in them.
My flesh is food indeed, and my blood is drink indeed,
says the Lord.

6

Whoever eats this bread will live for ever.
Whoever eats this bread will live for ever.
This is the true bread which comes down from heaven
and gives life to the world.
Whoever eats this bread will live for ever.

Whoever believes in me shall not hunger or thirst,
for the bread which I give for the life of the world
is my flesh.
Whoever eats this bread will live for ever.

Anthems 7 through 10 are not used in the season of Lent.

7

Alleluia. Christ our Passover is sacrificed for us;
Therefore let us keep the feast. Alleluia.

8

Alleluia.
Alleluia.
Christ our Passover is sacrificed for us;
therefore let us keep the feast.
Alleluia.

9

The disciples knew the Lord Jesus
in the breaking of the bread.
The disciples knew the Lord Jesus
in the breaking of the bread.
The bread which we break, alleluia,
is the communion of the body of Christ.
The disciples knew the Lord Jesus
in the breaking of the bread.
One body are we, alleluia,
for though many we share one bread.
The disciples knew the Lord Jesus
in the breaking of the bread.

10

Be known to us, Lord Jesus, in the breaking of the bread.
Be known to us, Lord Jesus, in the breaking of the bread.
The bread which we break, alleluia,
is the communion of the body of Christ.
Be known to us, Lord Jesus, in the breaking of the bread.
One body are we, alleluia,
for though many we share one bread.
Be known to us, Lord Jesus, in the breaking of the bread.

The following anthems may be used as separate pieces, or as refrains with selected verses from the psalms. In Easter Season, it is appropriate to add Alleluia (Hallelujah) to the anthem or refrain.

11

Blessed are those who are called to the Supper of the Lamb.

12

Whoever comes to me shall not hunger, and whoever believes in me shall never thirst.

13

Those who eat my flesh and drink my blood abide in me and I in them.

14

You shall eat and drink at my table in my kingdom, says the Lord.

15

Christ our Passover is sacrificed for us; therefore let us keep the feast.

Suggested Psalm Verses

Advent   Psalm 85:8-11

Christmas – 1 Epiphany   Psalm 96:8-11
                            Psalm 110:1-4

Lent   Psalm 106:4-5
          Psalm 108:3-6

Easter   Psalm 107:1-3, 8
            Psalm 116:10-11, 16-17

General   Psalm 34:3 & 8
             Psalm 43:3-4
             Psalm 103:1-4
             Psalm 105:1-4
             Psalm 117

Seasonal Blessings

The following blessings may be used by a bishop or priest whenever a blessing is appropriate.

Two forms of blessing are provided for each major season (except for Lent). The first is a three-fold form, with an Amen at the end of each sentence, leading into a trinitarian blessing. The second is a single-sentence formula leading directly into the blessing.

The formula for chanting these blessings is given in the musical appendix to the Altar Edition.

Advent

May Almighty God, by whose providence our Savior Christ came among us in great humility, sanctify you with the light of his blessing and set you free from all sin. *Amen.*

May he whose second Coming in power and great glory we await, make you steadfast in faith, joyful in hope, and constant in love. *Amen.*

May you, who rejoice in the first Advent of our Redeemer, at his second Advent be rewarded with unending life. *Amen.*

And the blessing of God Almighty, the Father, the Son, and the Holy Spirit, be upon you and remain with you for ever. *Amen.*

or this

May the Sun of Righteousness shine upon you and scatter the darkness from before your path; and the blessing of God Almighty, the Father, the Son, and the Holy Spirit, be among you, and remain with you always. *Amen.*

Christmas Season

May Almighty God, who sent his Son to take our nature upon him, bless you in this holy season, scatter the darkness of sin, and brighten your heart with the light of his holiness. *Amen.*

May God, who sent his angels to proclaim the glad news of the Savior's birth, fill you with joy, and make you heralds of the Gospel. *Amen.*

May God, who in the Word made flesh joined heaven to earth and earth to heaven, give you his peace and favor. *Amen.*

And the blessing of God Almighty, the Father, the Son, and the Holy Spirit, be upon you and remain with you for ever. *Amen.*

or this

May Christ, who by his Incarnation gathered into one things earthly and heavenly, fill you with his joy and peace; and the blessing of God Almighty, the Father, the Son, and the Holy Spirit, be among you, and remain with you always. *Amen.*

Epiphany

For use from the feast of the Epiphany through the following Sunday; and on the Second Sunday after the Epiphany in Year C.

May Almighty God, who led the Wise Men by the shining of a star to find the Christ, the Light from Light, lead you also, in your pilgrimage, to find the Lord. *Amen.*

May God, who sent the Holy Spirit to rest upon the Only-begotten at his baptism in the Jordan River, pour out that Spirit on you who have come to the waters of new birth. *Amen.*

May God, by the power that turned water into wine at the wedding feast at Cana, transform your lives and make glad your hearts. *Amen.*

And the blessing of God Almighty, the Father, the Son, and the Holy Spirit, be upon you and remain with you for ever. *Amen.*

or this

May Christ, the Son of God, be manifest in you, that your lives may be a light to the world; and the blessing of God Almighty, the Father, the Son, and the Holy Spirit, be among you, and remain with you always. *Amen.*

Lent

In Lent, in place of a seasonal blessing, a solemn Prayer over the People is used, as follows:

The Deacon or, in the absence of a deacon, the Celebrant says

Bow down before the Lord.

The people kneel and the Celebrant says one of the following prayers:

1

Grant, most merciful Lord, to your faithful people pardon
and peace, that they may be cleansed from all their sins, and
serve you with a quiet mind; through Christ our Lord.
Amen.

2

Grant, Almighty God, that your people may recognize their
weakness and put their whole trust in your strength, so that
they may rejoice for ever in the protection of your loving
providence; through Christ our Lord. *Amen.*

3

Keep this your family, Lord, with your never-failing mercy,
that relying solely on the help of your heavenly grace, they
may be upheld by your divine protection; through Christ our
Lord. *Amen.*

4

Look mercifully on this your family, Almighty God, that by
your great goodness they may be governed and preserved
evermore; through Christ our Lord. *Amen.*

5

Look down in mercy, Lord, on your people who kneel before
you; and grant that those whom you have nourished by your
Word and Sacraments may bring forth fruit worthy of
repentance; through Christ our Lord. *Amen.*

6

Look with compassion, O Lord, upon this your people; that, rightly observing this holy season, they may learn to know you more fully, and to serve you with a more perfect will; through Christ our Lord. *Amen.*

From Palm Sunday through Maundy Thursday

Almighty God, we pray you graciously to behold this your family, for whom our Lord Jesus Christ was willing to be betrayed, and given into the hands of sinners, and to suffer death upon the cross; who lives and reigns for ever and ever. *Amen.*

Easter Season

May Almighty God, who has redeemed us and made us his children through the resurrection of his Son our Lord, bestow upon you the riches of his blessing. *Amen.*

May God, who through the water of baptism has raised us from sin into newness of life, make you holy and worthy to be united with Christ for ever. *Amen.*

May God, who has brought us out of bondage to sin into true and lasting freedom in the Redeemer, bring you to your eternal inheritance. *Amen.*

And the blessing of God Almighty, the Father, the Son, and the Holy Spirit, be upon you and remain with you for ever. *Amen.*

or this

The God of peace, who brought again from the dead our Lord Jesus Christ, the great Shepherd of the sheep, through the blood of the everlasting covenant, make you perfect in every good work to do his will, working in you that which is well-pleasing in his sight; and the blessing of God Almighty, the Father, the Son, and the Holy Spirit, be among you, and remain with you always. *Amen.*

The Day of Pentecost

May Almighty God, who enlightened the minds of the disciples by pouring out upon them the Holy Spirit, make you rich with his blessing, that you may abound more and more in that Spirit for ever. *Amen.*

May God, who sent the Holy Spirit as a flame of fire that rested upon the heads of the disciples, burn out all evil from your hearts, and make them shine with the pure light of his presence. *Amen.*

May God, who by the Holy Spirit caused those of many tongues to proclaim Jesus as Lord, strengthen your faith and send you out to bear witness to him in word and deed. *Amen.*

And the blessing of God Almighty, the Father, the Son, and the Holy Spirit, be upon you and remain with you for ever. *Amen.*

or this

May the Spirit of truth lead you into all truth, giving you grace to confess that Jesus Christ is Lord, and to proclaim the wonderful works of God; and the blessing of God Almighty, the Father, the Son, and the Holy Spirit, be among you, and remain with you always. *Amen.*

The First Sunday after Pentecost: Trinity Sunday

The Lord bless you and keep you. *Amen.*

The Lord make his face to shine upon you, and be gracious to you. *Amen.*

The Lord lift up his countenance upon you, and give you peace. *Amen.*

The Lord God Almighty, Father, Son, and Holy Spirit, the holy and undivided Trinity, guard you, save you, and bring you to that heavenly City, where he lives and reigns for ever and ever. *Amen.*

or this

May God the Holy Trinity make you strong in faith and love, defend you on every side, and guide you in truth and peace; and the blessing of God Almighty, the Father, the Son, and the Holy Spirit, be among you, and remain with you always. *Amen.*

All Saints

May Almighty God, to whose glory we celebrate this festival of all the Saints, be now and evermore your guide and companion in the way. *Amen.*

May God, who has bound us together in the company of the elect, in this age and the age to come, attend to the prayers of his faithful servants on your behalf, as he hears your prayers for them. *Amen.*

May God, who has given us, in the lives of his saints, patterns of holy living and victorious dying, strengthen your faith and devotion, and enable you to bear witness to the truth against all adversity. *Amen.*

And the blessing of God Almighty, the Father, the Son, and the Holy Spirit, be upon you and remain with you for ever. *Amen.*

The preceding blessing may be adapted for use at a Patronal Festival.

or this

May God give you grace to follow his saints in faith and hope and love; and the blessing of God Almighty, the Father, the Son, and the Holy Spirit, be among you, and remain with you always. *Amen.*

Concerning the Advent Wreath

The Advent Wreath is a visual symbol marking the progress of the season of Advent. When it used in the church, no special prayers or ceremonial elaboration beyond what is described on page 143 of the Prayer Book is desirable. At morning services the appropriate number of candles is lighted before the service begins.

When used in private homes, the Advent Wreath provides a convenient focus for devotions at the time of the evening meal. The short form of An Order of Worship for the Evening, Prayer Book pages 109-112, is recommended.

In place of the Short Lesson of Scripture provided in the Order, one of the readings from the Daily Office Lectionary may be used, in whole or in part. Alternatively, some other plan of Bible reading may be followed.

Phos hilaron is always appropriate but an Advent hymn may be substituted for it.

Advent Festival
of Lessons and Music

The following bidding and lessons may be used at a festival held in Advent.

If the festival takes place in the evening, it may be introduced by the Service of Light (Prayer Book, page 109). The seasonal Lucernarium (page 10) or Psalm 85:7-13 may be sung during the candle lighting. After the Phos hilaron or the hymn sung in place of it, the service continues with the Bidding Prayer.

A Bidding Prayer   *Traditional*

Beloved in Christ, in this season of Advent, let it be our care and delight to prepare ourselves to hear again the message of the Angels, and in heart and mind to go even unto Bethlehem, to see the Babe lying in a manger.

Let us read and mark in Holy Scripture the tale of the loving purposes of God from the first days of our disobedience unto the glorious Redemption brought us by his holy Child; and let us look forward to the yearly remembrance of his birth with hymns and songs of praise.

But first, let us pray for the needs of his whole world; for peace and goodwill over all the earth; for the mission and unity of the Church for which he died, and especially in this country and within this *city*.

And because this of all things would rejoice his heart, let us at this time remember in his name the poor and the helpless; the hungry and the oppressed; the sick and those who mourn; the lonely and the unloved; the aged and the little children; and all those who know not the Lord Jesus, or who love him not, or who by sin have grieved his heart of love.

Lastly, let us remember before God his pure and lowly Mother, and all those who rejoice with us, but upon another shore and in a greater light, that multitude which no one can number, whose hope was in the Word made flesh, and with whom, in this Lord Jesus, we for evermore are one.

These prayers and praises let us humbly offer up to the throne of heaven, in the words which Christ himself hath taught us:

Our Father . . . .

The Almighty God bless us with his grace; Christ give us the joys of everlasting life; and unto the fellowship of the citizens above may the King of Angels bring us all. *Amen.*

A Bidding Prayer *Contemporary*

Dear People of God: In the season of Advent, it is our responsibility and joy to prepare ourselves to hear once more the message of the Angels, to go to Bethlehem and see the Son of God lying in a manger.

Let us hear and heed in Holy Scripture the story of God's loving purpose from the time of our rebellion against him until the glorious redemption brought to us by his holy Child Jesus, and let us look forward to the yearly remembrance of his birth with hymns and songs of praise.

But first, let us pray for the needs of his whole world, for peace and justice on earth, for the unity and mission of the Church for which he died, and especially for his Church in our country and in this *city*.

And because he particularly loves them, let us remember in his name the poor and helpless, the cold, the hungry and the oppressed, the sick and those who mourn, the lonely and unloved, the aged and little children, as well as all those who do not know and love the Lord Jesus Christ.

Finally, let us remember before God his pure and lowly Mother, and that whole multitude which no one can number, whose hope was in the Word made flesh, and with whom, in Jesus, we are one for evermore.

And now, to sum up all these petitions, let us pray in the words which Christ himself has taught us, saying:

Our Father . . . .

The Almighty God bless us with his grace; Christ give us the joys of everlasting life; and to the fellowship of the citizens above may the King of Angels bring us all. *Amen.*

The Lessons

Nine Lessons are customarily selected (but fewer may be used), interspersed with appropriate Advent hymns, canticles, and anthems. When possible, each Lesson is read by a different lector. The Lesson from the third chapter of Genesis is never omitted.

The Lessons may be read without announcement or conclusion, or in the manner prescribed in the Daily Office. A period of silence may follow each Lesson.

Genesis 2:4b-9, 15-25 (God creates man and woman to live in obedience to him in the Garden of Eden)

Genesis 3:1-22 *or* 3:1-15 (Adam and Eve rebel against God and are cast out of the Garden of Eden)

Isaiah 40:1-11 (God comforts his people and calls on them to prepare for redemption)

Jeremiah 31:31-34 (A new covenant is promised which will be written in our hearts)

Isaiah 64:1-9a (God is called upon to act and to come among us)

Isaiah 6:1-11 (God reveals his glory to the prophet and calls him to be his messenger)

Isaiah 35:1-10 (The prophet proclaims that God will come and save us)

Baruch 4:36—5:9 (The Scribe Baruch urges the people to look East because salvation is at hand)

Isaiah 7:10-15 (God promises that a child shall be conceived who will be known as "God with us")

Micah 5:2-4 (The one who is to rule Israel will be born in the village of Bethlehem)

Isaiah 11:1-9 (The Spirit of the Lord will rest upon the Holy One)

Zephaniah 3:14-18 (The Lord will be among us; we are summoned to rejoice and sing)

Isaiah 65:17-25 (God promises a new heaven and a new earth)

If it is desired that the Lessons end with a reading from the Gospel, one of the following may be used:

Luke 1:5-25 (An angel announces to Zechariah that his wife Elizabeth will bear a son)

Luke 1:26-38 *or* 1:26-56 (The Angel Gabriel announces to the Virgin Mary that she will bear the Son of the Most High)

The service may conclude with an appropriate Collect and the seasonal blessing for Advent.

A sermon is not a traditional part of this service.

Vigil for Christmas Eve

If it is desired to preface the midnight Eucharist of Christmas by a vigil, the following form may be used.

The rite begins with the Service of Light, page 109 of the Prayer Book, using the Collect of the First Sunday after Christmas Day as the Prayer for Light. During the candle lighting, the seasonal Lucernarium (page 10) or Psalm 113 may be sung. The Magnificat or a suitable hymn, such as "Of the Father's love begotten," may be substituted for Phos hilaron.

After the hymn, a series of biblical passages is read (see pages 38-39 for suggestions), interspersed with anthems, canticles, hymns, carols, or instrumental music. A period of silent reflection may follow each Reading.

After the last reading, there may be a procession to the creche, where a suitable prayer is said. (See the next page.)

The procession then continues to the chancel, and the Eucharist begins in the usual way.

Station at a Christmas Creche

At their entry into the church for the celebration of the Holy Eucharist, the Celebrant (and other ministers) may make a station at a Christmas Creche. The figure of the Christ Child may be carried in the procession and placed in the creche. Other figures may also be brought in if desired.

A versicle may be said, and one of the prayers which follow.

V. The word was made flesh and dwelt among us:
R. And we beheld his glory.

or this

V. The glory of the Lord has been revealed:
R. And all flesh shall see the salvation of our God.

Let us pray.

Almighty and everliving God, you have given us a new revelation of your loving providence in the Coming of your Son Jesus Christ to be born of the Virgin Mary: Grant that as he shared our mortality, so we may share his eternity in the glory of your kingdom; where he lives and reigns for ever and ever. *Amen.*

or the following

O God our Creator, to restore our fallen race you spoke the effectual word, and the Eternal Word became flesh in the womb of the Blessed Virgin Mary: Mercifully grant that as he humbled himself to be clothed with our humanity, so we may be found worthy, in him, to be clothed with his divinity; who lives and reigns for ever and ever. *Amen.*

or this

Most merciful and loving God, you have made this day holy by the incarnation of your Son Jesus Christ, and by the child-bearing of the Blessed Virgin Mary: Grant that we your people may enter with joy into the celebration of this day, and may also rejoice for ever as your adopted sons and daughters; through Jesus Christ our Lord. *Amen.*

Any of the Collects for Christmas Season may be used instead.

Christmas Festival
of Lessons and Music

The following bidding and lessons may be used at a festival during the Twelve Days of Christmas.

If the festival takes place in the evening, it may be introduced by the Service of Light (Prayer Book, page 109). The seasonal Lucernarium (page 10) or Psalm 113 may be sung during the candle lighting. After the Phos hilaron or the hymn sung in place of it, the service continues with the Bidding Prayer.

A Bidding Prayer   *Traditional*

Beloved in Christ, in this Christmastide, let it be our care and delight to hear again the message of the Angels, and in heart and mind to go even unto Bethlehem, and see this thing which is come to pass, and the Babe lying in a manger.

Let us read and mark in Holy Scripture the tale of the loving purposes of God from the first days of our disobedience unto the glorious Redemption brought us by this holy Child; and let us make this *place* glad with our carols of praise.

But first, let us pray for the needs of his whole world; for peace and goodwill over all the earth; for the mission and unity of the Church for which he died, and especially in this country and within this *city*.

And because this of all things would rejoice his heart, let us at this time remember in his name the poor and the helpless; the hungry and the oppressed; the sick and those who mourn; the lonely and the unloved; the aged and the little children; and all those who know not the Lord Jesus, or who love him not, or who by sin have grieved his heart of love.

Lastly, let us remember before God his pure and lowly Mother, and all those who rejoice with us, but upon another shore and in a greater light, that multitude which no one can number, whose hope was in the Word made flesh, and with whom, in this Lord Jesus, we for evermore are one.

These prayers and praises let us humbly offer up to the throne of heaven, in the words which Christ himself hath taught us:

Our Father . . . .

The Almighty God bless us with his grace; Christ give us the joys of everlasting life; and unto the fellowship of the citizens above may the King of Angels bring us all. *Amen.*

A Bidding Prayer *Contemporary*

Dear People of God: In this Christmas Season, let it be our duty and delight to hear once more the message of the Angels, to go to Bethlehem and see the Son of God lying in a manger.

Let us hear and heed in Holy Scripture the story of God's loving purpose from the time of our rebellion against him until the glorious redemption brought to us by his holy Child Jesus, and let us make this *place* glad with our carols of praise.

But first, let us pray for the needs of his whole world, for peace and justice on earth, for the unity and mission of the Church for which he died, and especially for his Church in our country and in this *city*.

And because he particularly loves them, let us remember in his name the poor and helpless, the cold, the hungry and the oppressed, the sick and those who mourn, the lonely and unloved, the aged and little children, as well as all those who do not know and love the Lord Jesus Christ.

Finally, let us remember before God his pure and lowly Mother, and that whole multitude which no one can number, whose hope was in the Word made flesh, and with whom, in Jesus, we are one for evermore.

And now, to sum up all these petitions, let us pray in the words which Christ himself has taught us, saying:

Our Father . . . .

The Almighty God bless us with his grace; Christ give us the joys of everlasting life; and to the fellowship of the citizens above, may the King of Angels bring us all. *Amen.*

The Lessons

Nine Lessons are customarily selected (but fewer may be used), interspersed with appropriate carols, hymns, canticles, and anthems. When possible, each lesson is read by a different lector. The lesson from the third chapter of Genesis is never omitted.

The Lessons may be read without announcement or conclusion, or in the manner prescribed in the Daily Office.

Genesis 2:4b-9, 15-25 (God creates man and woman to live in obedience to him in the Garden of Eden)
Genesis 3:1-23 *or* 3:1-15 (Adam and Eve rebel against God and are cast out of the Garden of Eden)

Isaiah 40:1-11 (God comforts his people and calls on them to prepare for redemption)

Isaiah 35:1-10 (The prophet proclaims that God will come and save us)

Isaiah 7:10-15 (God promises that a child shall be conceived who will be known as "God with us")

Luke 1:5-25 (An angel announces to Zechariah that his wife Elizabeth will bear a son)

Luke 1:26-58 (The Angel Gabriel announces to the Virgin Mary that she will bear the Son of the Most High)

Luke 1:39-46 *or* 1:39-56 (The Virgin Mary is greeted by Elizabeth and proclaims her joy)

Luke 1:57-80 (John the Baptist is born and his father rejoices that his son will prepare the way of the Lord)

Luke 2:1-20 (Jesus is born at Bethlehem and is worshiped by angels and shepherds)

Luke 2:21-36 (Jesus receives his name and is presented to Simeon in the Temple)

Hebrews 1:1-12 (In the fullness of time, God sent his Son whose reign is for ever and ever)

John 1:1-18 (The Word was made flesh and we have seen his glory)

The service may conclude with a suitable Collect and the seasonal blessing for Christmas.

A sermon is not a traditional part of this service.

Service for New Year's Eve

During the evening of December 31, which is the eve of the Feast of the Holy Name and also the eve of the civil New Year, the following service may be used.

The rite begins with the Service of Light, page 109 of the Prayer Book, using the Collect for the First Sunday after Christmas as the Prayer for Light.

After the Phos hilaron, two or more of the following Lessons are read, each followed by a Psalm, Canticle, or hymn, and a Prayer. The last reading is always from the New Testament.

The Hebrew Year
Exodus 23:9-16, 20-21

Psalm 111, *or* Psalm 119:1-8

Let us pray. *(Silence)*

O God our Creator, you have divided our life into days and seasons, and called us to acknowledge your providence year after year: Accept your people who come to offer their praises, and, in your mercy, receive their prayers; through Jesus Christ our Lord. *Amen.*

The Promised Land
Deuteronomy 11:8-12, 26-28

Psalm 36:5-10,   *or*   Psalm 89, Part I

Let us pray.   *(Silence)*

Almighty God, the source of all life, giver of all blessing, and savior of all who turn to you: Have mercy upon this nation; deliver us from falsehood, malice, and disobedience; turn our feet into your paths; and grant that we may serve you in peace; through Jesus Christ our Lord. *Amen.*

A Season for all Things
Ecclesiastes 3:1-15

Psalm 90

Let us pray.   *(Silence)*

In your wisdom, O Lord our God, you have made all things, and have allotted to each of us the days of our life: Grant that we may live in your presence, be guided by your Holy Spirit, and offer all our works to your honor and glory; through Jesus Christ our Lord. *Amen.*

Remember your Creator
Ecclesiastes 12:1-8

Psalm 130

Let us pray.   *(Silence)*

Immortal Lord God, you inhabit eternity, and have brought us your unworthy servants to the close of another year: Pardon, we entreat you, our transgressions of the past, and graciously abide with us all the days of our life; through Jesus Christ our Lord. *Amen.*

Marking the Times, and Winter
Ecclesiasticus 43:1-22

Psalm 19,   *or*   Psalm 148,   *or*   Psalm 74:11-22

Let us pray.   *(Silence)*

Almighty Father, you give the sun for a light by day, and the moon and the stars by night: Graciously receive us, this night and always, into your favor and protection, defending us from all harm and governing us with your Holy Spirit, that every shadow of ignorance, every failure of faith or weakness of heart, every evil or wrong desire may be removed far from us; so that we, being justified in our Lord Jesus Christ, may be sanctified by your Spirit, and glorified by your infinite mercies in the day of the glorious appearing of our Lord and Savior Jesus Christ. *Amen.*

The Acceptable Time
2 Corinthians 5:17—6:2

Psalm 63:1-8,   *or*   Canticle 5 or 17

Let us pray.   *(Silence)*

Most gracious and merciful God, you have reconciled us to yourself through Jesus Christ your Son, and called us to new life in him: Grant that we, who begin this year in his Name, may complete it to his honor and glory; who lives and reigns now and for ever. *Amen.*

While it is Called Today
Hebrews 3:1-15 (16—4:13)

Psalm 95

Let us pray.   *(Silence)*

O God, through your Son you have taught us to be watchful, and to await the sudden day of judgment: Strengthen us against Satan and his forces of wickedness, the evil powers of this world, and the sinful desires within us; and grant that, having served you all the days of our life, we may finally come to the dwelling place your Son has prepared for us; who lives and reigns for ever and ever. *Amen.*

New Heavens and New Earth
Revelation 21:1-14, 22-24

Canticle 19

Let us pray.   *(Silence)*

Almighty and merciful God, through your well beloved Son Jesus Christ, the King of kings and Lord of lords, you have willed to make all things new: Grant that we may be renewed by your Holy Spirit, and may come at last to that heavenly country where your people hunger and thirst no more, and the tears are wiped away from every eye; through Jesus Christ our Lord. *Amen.*

A homily, sermon, or instruction may follow the Readings.

An act of self-dedication may follow.

The service may conclude in one of the following ways:

1. *With the recitation of the Great Litany or some other form of intercession.*

2. *With the singing of Te Deum laudamus or some other hymn of praise, followed by the Lord's Prayer, the Collect for Holy Name, and a blessing or dismissal, or both.*

3. *With the Eucharist, beginning with the Gloria in excelsis or some other song of praise. The Proper for the Feast of the Holy Name is used.*

Blessing in Homes
at Epiphany

Where it is customary to invite the parish priest to the homes of parishioners on the Feast of the Epiphany or during the week following, this blessing may be used.

The Celebrant begins with the following or some other greeting

Peace be to this house, and to all who dwell in it.

The Magnificat is then sung or said with one of the following antiphons:

The Lord has shown forth his glory: Come let us adore him.

or this

I saw water proceeding out of the temple; from the right side it flowed, alleluia; and all those to whom that water came shall be saved, and shall say, alleluia, alleluia.

My soul proclaims the greatness of the Lord,
my spirit rejoices in God my Savior; *
    for he has looked with favor on his lowly servant.
From this day all generations will call me blessed: *
    the Almighty has done great things for me,
    and holy is his Name.
He has mercy on those who fear him *
    in every generation.

He has shown the strength of his arm, *
　　he has scattered the proud in their conceit.
He has cast down the mighty from their thrones. *
　　and has lifted up the lowly.
He has filled the hungry with good things, *
　　and the rich he has sent away empty.
He has come to the help of his servant Israel, *
　　for he has remembered his promise of mercy,
The promise he made to our fathers, *
　　to Abraham and his children for ever.
Glory to the Father, and to the Son, and to the Holy Spirit: *
　　as it was in the beginning, is now, and will be for ever. Amen.

The antiphon is then repeated.

Celebrant　The Lord be with you.
People　　And also with you.
Celebrant　Let us pray.

The Celebrant says one of the following Collects:

O God, by the leading of a star you manifested your only
Son to the peoples of the earth: Lead us, who know you now
by faith, to your presence, where we may see your glory face
to face; through Jesus Christ our Lord, who lives and reigns
with you and the Holy Spirit, one God, now and for ever.
Amen.

or this

Father in heaven, who at the baptism of Jesus in the River
Jordan proclaimed him your beloved Son and anointed him
with the Holy Spirit: Grant that all who are baptized into his
Name may keep the covenant they have made, and boldly
confess him as Lord and Savior; who with you and the Holy
Spirit lives and reigns, one God, in glory everlasting. *Amen.*

The Celebrant then says this prayer

Visit, O blessed Lord, this home with the gladness of your presence, Bless *all* who *live* here with the gift of your love; and grant that *they* may manifest your love [to each other and] to all whose lives *they touch*. May *they* grow in grace and in the knowledge and love of you; guide, comfort, and strengthen *them*; and preserve *them* in peace, O Jesus Christ, now and for ever. *Amen.*

Other suitable prayers may be added.

The Celebrant may say one of the two following blessings:

May God the Father, who by Baptism adopts us as his children, grant you grace. *Amen.*

May God the Son, who sanctified a home at Nazareth, fill you with love. *Amen.*

May God the Holy Spirit, who has made the Church one family, keep you in peace. *Amen.*

or this

May Almighty God, who led the Wise Men by the shining of a star to find the Christ, the Light from Light, lead you also in your pilgrimage, to find the Lord. *Amen.*

May God, who sent the Holy Spirit to rest upon the Only-begotten at his baptism in the Jordan River, pour out that Spirit on you who have come to the waters of new birth. *Amen.*

May God, by the power that turned water into wine at the wedding feast at Cana, transform your lives and make glad your hearts. *Amen.*

And the blessing of God Almighty, the Father, the Son, and the Holy Spirit, be upon you and remain with you for ever. *Amen*.

The Peace may then be exchanged.

Vigil for the Eve
of the Baptism of Our Lord

*When a Vigil of the Baptism of the Lord is observed, it begins with the
Service of Light, page 109 of the Prayer Book (substituting, if desired,
the Gloria in excelsis for the Phos hilaron), and continues with the
Salutation and Collect of the Day. Three or more Lessons are read before
the Gospel, each followed by a period of silence and a Psalm, Canticle,
or hymn. Holy Baptism or Confirmation (beginning with the
Presentation of the Candidates), or the Renewal of Baptismal Vows,
Prayer Book page 292, follows the Sermon.*

The Story of the Flood
Genesis (7:1-5,11-18); 8:6-18; 9:8-13

Psalm 25:3-9, *or* Psalm 46

The Lord who Makes a Way in the Sea
Isaiah 43:15-19

Psalm 114

The Washing and Anointing of Aaron
Leviticus 8:1-12

Psalm 23 *or* Psalm 133

The Anointing of David
1 Samuel 16:1-13

Psalm 2:1-8 *or* Psalm 110:1-5

The Cleansing of Naaman in the Jordan
2 Kings 5:1-14

Psalm 51:8-13

Salvation Offered Freely to All
Isaiah 55:1-11

Canticle 9, The First Song of Isaiah

A new Heart and a new Spirit
Ezekiel 36:24-28

Psalm 42

The Spirit of the Lord is Upon Me
Isaiah 61:1-9

or   **Behold my Servant** *
      Isaiah 42:1-9

Psalm 89:20-29 *

When God's Patience Waited in the Days of Noah
1 Peter 3:15b-22

or   **God Anointed Jesus with the Holy Spirit** *
      Acts 10:34-38

The Baptism of Jesus *
Year A: Matthew 3:13-17
Year B: Mark 1:7-11
Year C: Luke 3:15-16,21-22

or   **The Resurrection and the Great Commission**
      Matthew 28:1-10, 16-20

*Proper Readings and Psalm for the Eucharist of the Feast

Candlemas Procession

This procession is intended for use immediately before the Holy Eucharist on the Feast of the Presentation of Our Lord in the Temple.

When circumstances permit, the congregation gathers at a place apart from the church so that all may go into the church in procession. If necessary, however, the procession takes place within the church. In this case it is suitable that the celebrant begin the rite standing just inside the door of the church.

All are provided with unlighted candles. A server holds the celebrant's candle until the procession begins. The congregation stands facing the celebrant.

The Celebrant greets the people with these words

> Light and peace, in Jesus Christ our Lord.
People   Thanks be to God.

The following canticle is then sung or said, during which the candles are lighted.

A Light to enlighten the nations,
and the glory of your people Israel.
A Light to enlighten the nations,
and the glory of your people Israel.

Lord, you now have set your servant free *
    to go in peace as you have promised.
A *Light to enlighten the nations,*
and the glory of your people Israel.

For these eyes of mine have seen the Savior, *
    whom you have prepared for all the world to see.
A *Light to enlighten the nations,*
and the glory of your people Israel.

The Celebrant then says the following prayer

Let us pray.

God our Father, source of all light, today you revealed to the aged Simeon your light which enlightens the nations. Fill our hearts with the light of faith, that we who bear these candles may walk in the path of goodness, and come to the Light that shines for ever, your Son Jesus Christ our Lord. *Amen.*

The Procession

Deacon   Let us go forth in peace.
People   In the name of Christ. Amen.

During the procession, all carry lighted candles; and appropriate hymns, psalms, or anthems are sung.

At a suitable place, the procession may halt while the following or some other appropriate Collect is said

Let us pray.

O God, you have made this day holy by the presentation of your Son in the Temple, and by the purification of the Blessed Virgin Mary: Mercifully grant that we, who delight in her humble readiness to be the birth-giver of the Only-begotten, may rejoice for ever in our adoption as his sisters and brothers; through Jesus Christ our Lord. *Amen.*

The following antiphon and psalm is appropriate as the procession approaches the Altar

We have waited in silence on your loving-kindness, O Lord, in the midst of your temple. Your praise, like your Name, O God, reaches to the world's end; your right hand is full of justice.

Psalm 48:1-2, 10-13

In place of the long antiphon given above, this shorter form may be used with the appointed Psalm

We have waited on your loving-kindness, O Lord, in the midst of your temple.

On arrival in the sanctuary, the celebrant goes to the usual place, and the Eucharist begins with the Gloria in excelsis.

After the Collect of the Day, all extinguish their candles.

If desired, the candles of the congregation may be lighted again at the time of the dismissal, and borne by them as they leave the church.

Concerning the Service

The devotion known as the Way of the Cross is an adaptation to local usage of a custom widely observed by pilgrims to Jerusalem: the offering of prayer at a series of places in that city traditionally associated with our Lord's passion and death.

The number of stations, which at first varied widely, finally became fixed at fourteen. Of these, eight are based directly on events recorded in the Gospels. The remaining six (numbers 3, 4, 6, 7, 9, and 13) are based on inferences from the Gospel account or from pious legend. If desired, these six stations may be omitted.

The form which follows is appropriate either as a public service or as a private devotion, particularly on the Fridays of Lent, but it should not displace the Proper Liturgy of Good Friday.

Traditionally, the stations are made before a series of plain wooden crosses placed along the walls of the church or in some other convenient place. With each cross there is sometimes associated a pictorial representation of the event being commemorated.

The hymn Stabat Mater ("At the cross her station keeping") has frequently been associated with this service, but is not an integral part of it. Selected stanzas of this hymn may appropriately be sung at the entrance of the ministers, and (after the opening devotions before the Altar) as the procession approaches the first station.

In the form which follows, the Trisagion ("Holy God") is the chant recommended as the procession goes from station to station. Alternatively, the Trisagion may be used to conclude each station, and stanzas of appropriate hymns sung as the procession moves. It is appropriate that all present take part in the procession.

The officiant at the service, whether clerical or lay, customarily leads the opening versicle at each station and reads the concluding Collect. The Readings (and the versicles which follow) are appropriately assigned to other persons.

The Way of the Cross

A hymn or other song may be sung during the entrance of the ministers.

Opening Devotions

In the Name of the Father, and of the Son, and of the Holy Spirit. *Amen.*

Lord, have mercy.
Christ, have mercy.
Lord, have mercy.

Officiant and People

Our Father, who art in heaven,
   hallowed be thy Name,
   thy kingdom come,
   thy will be done,
     on earth as it is in heaven.
Give us this day our daily bread.
And forgive us our trespasses,
   as we forgive those
     who trespass against us.
And lead us not into temptation,
   but deliver us from evil.

Our Father in heaven,
   hallowed be your Name,
   your kingdom come,
   your will be done,
     on earth as in heaven.
Give us today our daily bread.
Forgive us our sins,
   as we forgive those
     who sin against us.
Save us from the time of trial,
   and deliver us from evil.

V. We will glory in the cross of our Lord Jesus Christ:
R. In whom is our salvation, our life and resurrection.

Let us pray. *(Silence)*

Assist us mercifully with your help, O Lord God of our salvation, that we may enter with joy upon the contemplation of those mighty acts, whereby you have given us life and immortality; through Jesus Christ our Lord. *Amen.*

The procession goes to the First Station.

First Station

Jesus is condemned to death

We adore you, O Christ, and we bless you:
Because by your holy cross you have redeemed the world.

As soon as it was morning, the chief priests, with the elders
and scribes, and the whole council, held a consultation; and
they bound Jesus and led him away and delivered him to
Pilate. And they all condemned him and said, "He deserves
to die." When Pilate heard these words, he brought Jesus out
and sat down on the judgment seat at a place called the
Pavement, but in the Hebrew, Gabbatha. Then he handed
Jesus over to them to be crucified.

V. God did not spare his own Son:
R. But delivered him up for us all.

Let us pray. *(Silence)*

Almighty God, whose most dear Son went not up to joy but
first he suffered pain, and entered not into glory before he
was crucified: Mercifully grant that we, walking in the way
of the cross, may find it none other than the way of life and
peace; through Jesus Christ your Son our Lord. *Amen.*

Holy God,
Holy and Mighty,
Holy Immortal One,
Have mercy upon us.

Second Station

Jesus takes up his Cross

We adore you, O Christ, and we bless you:
Because by your holy cross you have redeemed the world.

Jesus went out, bearing his own cross, to the place called the place of a skull, which is called in Hebrew, Golgotha. Although he was a Son, he learned obedience through what he suffered. Like a lamb he was led to the slaughter; and like a sheep that before its shearers is mute, so he opened not his mouth. Worthy is the Lamb who was slain, to receive power and riches and wisdom and strength and honor and glory and blessing.

V. The Lord has laid on him the iniquity of us all:
R. For the transgression of my people was he stricken.

Let us pray.   (*Silence*)

Almighty God, whose beloved Son willingly endured the agony and shame of the cross for our redemption: Give us courage to take up our cross and follow him; who lives and reigns for ever and ever. *Amen.*

Holy God,
Holy and Mighty,
Holy Immortal One,
Have mercy upon us.

Third Station

Jesus falls the first time

We adore you, O Christ, and we bless you:
Because by your holy cross you have redeemed the world.

Christ Jesus, though he was in the form of God, did not count equality with God a thing to be grasped; but emptied himself, taking the form of a servant, and was born in human likeness. And being found in human form he humbled himself and became obedient unto death, even death on a cross. Therefore God has highly exalted him, and bestowed on him the name which is above every name. Come, let us bow down, and bend the knee, and kneel before the Lord our Maker, for he is the Lord our God.

V.   Surely he has borne our griefs:
R.   And carried our sorrows.

Let us pray.   *(Silence)*

O God, you know us to be set in the midst of so many and great dangers, that by reason of the frailty of our nature we cannot always stand upright: Grant us such strength and protection as may support us in all dangers, and carry us through all temptations; through Jesus Christ our Lord. *Amen.*

Holy God,
Holy and Mighty,
Holy Immortal One,
Have mercy upon us.

Fourth Station

Jesus meets his afflicted mother

We adore you, O Christ, and we bless you:
Because by your holy cross you have redeemed the world.

To what can I liken you, to what can I compare you, O
daughter of Jerusalem? What likeness can I use to comfort
you, O virgin daughter of Zion? For vast as the sea is your
ruin. Blessed are those who mourn, for they shall be
comforted. The Lord will be your everlasting light, and your
days of mourning shall be ended.

V.   A sword will pierce your own soul also:
R.   And fill your heart with bitter pain.

Let us pray.   *(Silence)*

O God, who willed that in the passion of your Son a sword
of grief should pierce the soul of the Blessed Virgin Mary his
mother: Mercifully grant that your Church, having shared
with her in his passion, may be made worthy to share in the
joys of his resurrection; who lives and reigns for ever and
ever. *Amen.*

Holy God,
Holy and Mighty,
Holy Immortal One,
Have mercy upon us.

Fifth Station

The Cross is laid on Simon of Cyrene

We adore you, O Christ, and we bless you:
Because by your holy cross you have redeemed the world.

As they led Jesus away, they came upon a man of Cyrene, Simon by name, who was coming in from the country, and laid on him the cross to carry it behind Jesus. "If anyone would come after me, let him deny himself and take up his cross and follow me. Take my yoke upon you, and learn from me; for my yoke is easy, and my burden is light."

V. Whoever does not bear his own cross and come after me:
R. Cannot be my disciple.

Let us pray. *(Silence)*

Heavenly Father, whose blessed Son came not to be served but to serve: Bless all who, following in his steps, give themselves to the service of others; that with wisdom, patience, and courage, they may minister in his Name to the suffering, the friendless, and the needy; for the love of him who laid down his life for us, your Son our Savior Jesus Christ. *Amen.*

Holy God,
Holy and Mighty,
Holy Immortal One,
Have mercy upon us.

Sixth Station

A woman wipes the face of Jesus

We adore you, O Christ, and we bless you:
Because by your holy cross you have redeemed the world.

We have seen him without beauty or majesty, with no looks
to attract our eyes. He was despised and rejected by men; a
man of sorrows, and acquainted with grief; and as one from
whom men hide their faces, he was despised, and we
esteemed him not. His appearance was so marred, beyond
human semblance, and his form beyond that of the children
of men. But he was wounded for our transgressions, he was
bruised for our iniquities; upon him was the chastisement
that made us whole, and with his stripes we are healed.

V. Restore us, O Lord God of hosts:
R. Show the light of your countenance, and we shall
be saved.

Let us pray. *(Silence)*

O God, who before the passion of your only-begotten Son
revealed his glory upon the holy mountain: Grant to us that
we, beholding by faith the light of his countenance, may be
strengthened to bear our cross, and be changed into his
likeness from glory to glory; through Jesus Christ our Lord.
Amen.

Holy God,
Holy and Mighty,
Holy Immortal One,
Have mercy upon us.

Seventh Station

Jesus falls a second time

We adore you, O Christ, and we bless you:
Because by your holy cross you have redeemed the world.

Surely he has borne our griefs and carried our sorrows. All we like sheep have gone astray; we have turned every one to his own way; and the Lord has laid on him the iniquity of us all. He was oppressed, and he was afflicted, yet he opened not his mouth. For the transgression of my people was he stricken.

V. But as for me, I am a worm and no man:
R. Scorned by all and despised by the people.

Let us pray. *(Silence)*

Almighty and everliving God, in your tender love for the human race you sent your Son our Savior Jesus Christ to take upon him our nature, and to suffer death upon the cross, giving us the example of his great humility: Mercifully grant that we may walk in the way of his suffering, and also share in his resurrection; who lives and reigns for ever and ever. *Amen.*

Holy God,
Holy and Mighty,
Holy Immortal One,
Have mercy upon us.

Eighth Station

Jesus meets the women of Jerusalem

We adore you, O Christ, and we bless you:
Because by your holy cross you have redeemed the world.

There followed after Jesus a great multitude of the people, and among them were women who bewailed and lamented him. But Jesus turning to them said, "Daughters of Jerusalem, do not weep for me, but weep for yourselves and for your children."

V.   Those who sowed with tears:
R.   Will reap with songs of joy.

Let us pray.   *(Silence)*

Teach your Church, O Lord, to mourn the sins of which it is guilty, and to repent and forsake them; that, by your pardoning grace, the results of our iniquities may not be visited upon our children and our children's children; through Jesus Christ our Lord. *Amen.*

Holy God,
Holy and Mighty,
Holy Immortal One,
Have mercy upon us.

Ninth Station

Jesus falls a third time

We adore you, O Christ, and we bless you:
Because by your holy cross you have redeemed the world.

I am the man who has seen affliction under the rod of his wrath; he has driven and brought me into darkness without any light. He has besieged me and enveloped me with bitterness and tribulation; he has made me dwell in darkness like the dead of long ago. Though I call and cry for help, he shuts out my prayer. He has made my teeth grind on gravel, and made me cower in ashes. "Remember, O Lord, my affliction and bitterness, the wormwood and the gall!"

V. He was led like a lamb to the slaughter:
R. And like a sheep that before its shearers is mute,
so he opened not his mouth.

Let us pray. *(Silence)*

O God, by the passion of your blessed Son you made an instrument of shameful death to be for us the means of life: Grant us so to glory in the cross of Christ, that we may gladly suffer shame and loss for the sake of your Son our Savior Jesus Christ. *Amen.*

Holy God,
Holy and Mighty,
Holy Immortal One,
Have mercy upon us.

Tenth Station

Jesus is stripped of his garments

We adore you, O Christ, and we bless you:
Because by your holy cross you have redeemed the world.

When they came to a place called Golgotha (which means the place of a skull), they offered him wine to drink, mingled with gall; but when he tasted it, he would not drink it. And they divided his garments among them by casting lots. This was to fulfill the scripture which says, "They divided my garments among them; they cast lots for my clothing."

V.   They gave me gall to eat:
R.   And when I was thirsty they gave me vinegar to drink.

Let us pray.   *(Silence)*

Lord God, whose blessed Son our Savior gave his body to be whipped and his face to be spit upon: Give us grace to accept joyfully the sufferings of the present time, confident of the glory that shall be revealed; through Jesus Christ our Lord. *Amen.*

Holy God,
Holy and Mighty,
Holy Immortal One,
Have mercy upon us.

Eleventh Station

Jesus is nailed to the Cross

We adore you, O Christ, and we bless you:
Because by your holy cross you have redeemed the world.

When they came to the place which is called The Skull, there they crucified him; and with him they crucified two criminals, one on the right, the other on the left, and Jesus between them. And the scripture was fulfilled which says, "He was numbered with the transgressors."

V.   They pierce my hands and my feet:
R.   They stare and gloat over me.

Let us pray.   *(Silence)*

Lord Jesus Christ, you stretched out your arms of love on the hard wood of the cross that everyone might come within the reach of your saving embrace: So clothe us in your Spirit that we, reaching forth our hands in love, may bring those who do not know you to the knowledge and love of you; for the honor of your Name. *Amen.*

Holy God,
Holy and Mighty,
Holy Immortal One,
Have mercy upon us.

Twelfth Station

Jesus dies on the Cross

We adore you, O Christ, and we bless you:
Because by your holy cross you have redeemed the world.

When Jesus saw his mother, and the disciple whom he loved standing near, he said to his mother, "Woman, behold your son!" Then he said to the disciple, "Behold your mother!" And when Jesus had received the vinegar, he said, "It is finished!" And then, crying with a loud voice, he said, "Father, into your hands I commend my spirit." And he bowed his head, and handed over his spirit.

V.   Christ for us became obedient unto death:
R.   Even death on a cross.

Let us pray.   *(Silence)*

O God, who for our redemption gave your only-begotten Son to the death of the cross, and by his glorious resurrection delivered us from the power of our enemy: Grant us so to die daily to sin, that we may evermore live with him in the joy of his resurrection; who lives and reigns now and for ever. *Amen.*

Holy God,
Holy and Mighty,
Holy Immortal One,
Have mercy upon us.

Thirteenth Station

The body of Jesus is placed in the arms of his mother

We adore you, O Christ, and we bless you:
Because by your holy cross you have redeemed the world.

All you who pass by, behold and see if there is any sorrow like my sorrow. My eyes are spent with weeping; my soul is in tumult; my heart is poured out in grief because of the downfall of my people. "Do not call me Naomi (which means Pleasant), call me Mara (which means Bitter); for the Almighty has dealt very bitterly with me."

V.   Her tears run down her cheeks:
R.   And she has none to comfort her.

Let us pray.   *(Silence)*

Lord Jesus Christ, by your death you took away the sting of death: Grant to us your servants so to follow in faith where you have led the way, that we may at length fall asleep peacefully in you and wake up in your likeness; for your tender mercies' sake. *Amen.*

Holy God,
Holy and Mighty,
Holy Immortal One,
Have mercy upon us.

Fourteenth Station

Jesus is laid in the tomb

We adore you, O Christ, and we bless you:
Because by your holy cross you have redeemed the world.

When it was evening, there came a rich man from
Arimathea, named Joseph, who also was a disciple of
Jesus. He went to Pilate and asked for the body of Jesus.
Then Pilate ordered it to be given to him. And Joseph took
the body, and wrapped it in a clean linen shroud, and laid it
in his own new tomb, which he had hewn in the rock; and
he rolled a great stone to the door of the tomb.

V. You will not abandon me to the grave:
R. Nor let your holy One see corruption.

Let us pray. *(Silence)*

O God, your blessed Son was laid in a tomb in a garden, and
rested on the Sabbath day: Grant that we who have been
buried with him in the waters of baptism may find our
perfect rest in his eternal and glorious kingdom; where he
lives and reigns for ever and ever. *Amen.*

Holy God,
Holy and Mighty,
Holy Immortal One,
Have mercy upon us.

Concluding Prayers before the Altar

Savior of the world, by your cross and precious blood you have redeemed us:
Save us, and help us, we humbly beseech you, O Lord.

Let us pray.   *(Silence)*

We thank you, heavenly Father, that you have delivered us from the dominion of sin and death and brought us into the kingdom of your Son; and we pray that, as by his death he has recalled us to life, so by his love he may raise us to eternal joys; who lives and reigns with you, in the unity of the Holy Spirit, one God, now and for ever. *Amen.*

To Christ our Lord who loves us, and washed us in his own blood, and made us a kingdom of priests to serve his God and Father, to him be glory and dominion for ever and ever. *Amen.*

Concerning the Service

The name *Tenebrae* (the Latin word for "darkness" or "shadows") has for centuries been applied to the ancient monastic night and early morning services (Matins and Lauds) of the last three days of Holy Week, which in medieval times came to be celebrated on the preceding evenings.

Apart from the chant of the Lamentations (in which each verse is introduced by a letter of the Hebrew alphabet), the most conspicuous feature of the service is the gradual extinguishing of candles and other lights in the church until only a single candle, considered a symbol of our Lord, remains. Toward the end of the service this candle is hidden, typifying the apparent victory of the forces of evil. At the very end, a loud noise is made, symbolizing the earthquake at the time of the resurrection (Matthew 28:2), the hidden candle is restored to its place, and by its light all depart in silence.

In this book, provision is made for Tenebrae on Wednesday evening only, in order that the proper liturgies of Maundy Thursday and Good Friday may find their place as the principal services of those days. By drawing upon material from each of the former three offices of Tenebrae, this service provides an extended meditation upon, and a prelude to, the events in our Lord's life between the Last Supper and the Resurrection.

Additional Directions are on page 89.

Tenebrae

The ministers enter the church in silence and proceed to their places. The Office then begins immediately with the Antiphon on the first Psalm. It is customary to sit for the Psalmody.

First Nocturn

Antiphon 1

Zeal for your house has eaten me up; the scorn of those who scorn you has fallen upon me.

Psalm 69,   or   Psalm 69:1-23

Antiphon 2

Let them draw back and be disgraced who take pleasure in my misfortune.

Psalm 70

Antiphon 3

Arise, O God, maintain my cause.

Psalm 74

V. Deliver me, my God, from the hand of the wicked:
R. From the clutches of the evildoer and the oppressor.

All stand for silent prayer. The appointed Reader then goes to the lectern, and everyone else sits down.

Lesson 1

A Reading from the Lamentations of Jeremiah the Prophet. [1:1-14]

Aleph. How solitary lies the city, once so full of people! How like a widow has she become, she that was great among the nations! She that was queen among the cities has now become a vassal.

Beth. She weeps bitterly in the night, tears run down her cheeks; among all her lovers she has none to comfort her; all her friends have dealt treacherously with her; they have become her enemies.

Gimel. Judah has gone into the misery of exile and of hard servitude; she dwells now among the nations, but finds no resting place; all her pursuers overtook her in the midst of her anguish.

Daleth. The roads to Zion mourn, because none come to the solemn feasts; all her gates are desolate, her priests groan and sigh; her virgins are afflicted, and she is in bitterness.

He. Her adversaries have become her masters, her enemies prosper; because the Lord has punished her for the multitude of her rebellions; her children are gone, driven away as captives by the enemy.

Jerusalem, Jerusalem, return to the Lord your God!

Responsory 1 *In monte Oliveti*

On the mount of Olives Jesus prayed to the Father:
Father, if it be possible, let this cup pass from me.
The spirit indeed is willing, but the flesh is weak.
V.   Watch and pray, that you may not enter into temptation.
The spirit indeed is willing, but the flesh is weak.

Lesson 2

Waw. And from Daughter Zion all her majesty has departed;
her princes have become like stags that can find no pasture,
and that run without strength before the hunter.

Zayin. Jerusalem remembers in the days of her affliction and
bitterness all the precious things that were hers from the
days of old; when her people fell into the hand of the foe,
and there was none to help her; the adversary saw her, and
mocked at her downfall.

Heth. Jerusalem has sinned greatly, therefore she has become
a thing unclean; all who honored her despise her, for they
have seen her nakedness; and now she sighs, and turns her
face away.

Teth. Uncleanness clung to her skirts, she took no thought of
her doom; therefore her fall is terrible, she has no comforter.
"O Lord, behold my affliction, for the enemy has triumphed."

Jerusalem, Jerusalem, return to the Lord your God!

Responsory 2 *Tristis est anima mea*

My soul is very sorrowful, even to the point of death;
remain here, and watch with me.

Now you shall see the crowd who will surround me;
you will flee, and I will go to be offered up for you.
V.   Behold, the hour is at hand, and the Son of Man
      is betrayed into the hands of sinners.
You will flee, and I will go to be offered up for you.

Lesson 3

Yodh. The adversary has stretched out his hand to seize all
her precious things; she has seen the Gentiles invade her
sanctuary, those whom you had forbidden to enter your
congregation.

Kaph. All her people groan as they search for bread; they sell
their own children for food to revive their strength. "Behold,
O Lord, and consider, for I am now beneath contempt!"

Lamedh. Is it nothing to you, all you who pass by? Behold
and see if there is any sorrow like my sorrow, which was
brought upon me, which the Lord inflicted, on the day of his
burning anger.

Mem. From on high he sent fire, into my bones it descended;
he spread a net for my feet, and turned me back; he has left
me desolate and faint all the day long.

Nun. My transgressions were bound into a yoke; by his
hand they were fastened together; their yoke is upon my
neck; he has caused my strength to fail. The Lord has
delivered me into their hands, against whom I am not able to
stand up.

Jerusalem, Jerusalem, return to the Lord your God!

Responsory 3 *Ecce vidimus eum*

Lo, we have seen him without beauty or majesty,
with no looks to attract our eyes.
He bore our sins and grieved for us,
he was wounded for our transgressions,
and by his scourging we are healed.
V.   Surely he has borne our griefs and carried our sorrows:
And by his scourging we are healed.

When this Responsory is sung rather than recited, repeat all that
precedes the Verse:

Lo, we have seen . . . we are healed.

Second Nocturn

Antiphon 4

The kings of the earth rise up in revolt, and the princes plot
together, against the Lord and against his Anointed.

Psalm 2

Antiphon 5

They divide my garments among them; they cast lots for my
clothing.

Psalm 22,   or   Psalm 22:1-21

Antiphon 6

False witnesses have risen up against me, and also those who
speak malice.

Psalm 27

V. They divide my garments among them:
R. They cast lots for my clothing.

All stand for silent prayer. The appointed Reader then goes to the lectern, and everyone else sits down.

Lesson 4

A Reading from the Treatise of Saint Augustine the Bishop on the Psalms. [Vulgate Psalm 54. Prayer Book Psalm 55:1, 2, 10c]

"Hear my prayer, O God; do not hide yourself from my petition. Listen to me and answer me. I mourn in my trial and am troubled."

These are the words of one disquieted, in trouble and anxiety. He prays under much suffering, desiring to be delivered from evil. Let us now see under what evil he lies; and when he begins to speak, let us place ourselves beside him, that, by sharing his tribulation, we may also join in his prayer.

"I mourn in my trial," he says, "and am troubled."

When does he mourn? When is he troubled? He says, "In my trial." He has in mind the wicked who cause him suffering, and he calls this suffering his "trial." Do not think that the evil are in the world for no purpose, and that God makes no good use of them. Every wicked person lives either that he may be corrected, or that through him the righteous may be tried and tested.

Responsory 4 *Tamquam ad latronem*

Have you come out as against a robber,
with swords and clubs to capture me?

Day after day I sat in the temple teaching,
and you did not seize me;
but now, behold, you scourge me,
and lead me away to be crucified.
V.   When they had laid hands on Jesus and were holding
     him, he said:
Day after day I sat in the temple teaching,
and you did not seize me;
but now, behold, you scourge me,
and lead me away to be crucified.

Lesson 5

Would that those who now test us were converted and tried
with us; yet though they continue to try us, let us not hate
them, for we do not know whether any of them will persist
to the end in their evil ways. And most of the time, when you
think you are hating your enemy, you are hating your
brother without knowing it.

Only the devil and his angels are shown to us in the Holy
Scriptures as doomed to eternal fire. It is only their
amendment that is hopeless, and against them we wage a
hidden battle. For this battle the Apostle arms us, saying,
"We are not contending against flesh and blood," that is, not
against human beings whom we see, "but against the
principalities, against the powers, against the rulers of the
darkness of this world." So that you may not think that
demons are the rulers of heaven and earth, he says, "of the
darkness of this world."

He says, "of the world," meaning the lovers of the world —
of the "world," meaning the ungodly and wicked —
the "world" of which the Gospel says, "And the world
knew him not."

Responsory 5 *Tenebrae factae sunt*

Darkness covered the whole land
when Jesus had been crucified;
and about the ninth hour he cried with a loud voice:
My God, my God, why have you forsaken me?
And he bowed his head and handed over his spirit.
V.   Jesus, crying with a loud voice, said:
        Father, into your hands I commend my spirit.
And he bowed his head and handed over his spirit.

Lesson 6

"For I have seen unrighteousness and strife in the city."

See the glory of the cross itself. On the brow of kings that
cross is now placed, the cross which enemies once mocked.
Its power is shown in the result. He has conquered the
world, not by steel, but by wood. The wood of the cross
seemed a fitting object of scorn to his enemies, and standing
before that wood they wagged their heads, saying, "If you
are the Son of God, come down from the cross." He
stretched out his hands to an unbelieving and rebellious
people. If one is just who lives by faith, one who does not
have faith is unrighteous. Therefore when he says
"unrighteousness," understand that it is unbelief. The Lord
then saw unrighteousness and strife in the city, and stretched
out his hands to an unbelieving and rebellious people. And
yet, looking upon them, he said, "Father, forgive them, for
they know not what they do."

Responsory 6 *Ecce quomodo moritur*

See how the righteous one perishes,
and no one takes it to heart.

The righteous are taken away, and no one understands.
From the face of evil the righteous one is taken away,
and his memory shall be in peace.
V.   Like a sheep before its shearers is mute, so he opened
     not his mouth. By oppression and judgment he was
     taken away:
And his memory shall be in peace.

When this Responsory is sung rather than recited, repeat all that
precedes the Verse:

See how the righteous . . . in peace.

Third Nocturn

Antiphon 7

God is my helper; it is the Lord who sustains my life.

Psalm 54

Antiphon 8

At Salem is his tabernacle, and his dwelling is in Zion.

Psalm 76

Antiphon 9

I have become like one who has no strength, lost among the
dead.

Psalm 88

V.   He has made me dwell in darkness:
R.   Like the dead of long ago.

*All stand for silent prayer. The appointed Reader then goes to the
lectern, and everyone else sits down.*

Lesson 7

A Reading from the Letter to the Hebrews.
[4:15—5:10; 9:11-15a]

We do not have a high priest who is unable to sympathize
with our weaknesses, but one who in every respect has been
tempted as we are, yet without sinning. Let us then with
confidence draw near to the throne of grace, that we may
receive mercy and find grace to help in time of need. For
every high priest chosen from among men is appointed to act
on behalf of men in relation to God, to offer gifts and
sacrifices for sins. He can deal gently with the ignorant and
wayward, since he himself is beset with weakness. Because
of this he is bound to offer sacrifice for his own sins as well
as for those of the people.

Responsory 7 *Eram quasi agnus*

I was like a trusting lamb led to the slaughter.
I did not know it was against me
that they devised schemes, saying,
Let us destroy the tree with its fruit;
let us cut him off from the land of the living.
V.   All my enemies whispered together against me,
      and devised evil against me, saying:
Let us destroy the tree with its fruit;
let us cut him off from the land of the living.

Lesson 8

And one does not take the honor upon himself, but he is called by God, just as Aaron was. So also, Christ did not exalt himself to be made a high priest, but was appointed by him who said to him, "You are my Son, this day have I begotten you;" as he says also in another place, "You are a priest for ever after the order of Melchizedek." In the days of his flesh, Jesus offered up prayers and supplications, with loud cries and tears, to him who was able to save him from death, and he was heard for his godly fear. Although he was a Son, he learned obedience through what he suffered; and, being made perfect, he became the source of eternal salvation to all who obey him, being designated by God a high priest after the order of Melchizedek.

Responsory 8   *Velum templi*

The veil of the temple was torn in two,
and the earth shook, and the thief from the cross cried out,
Lord, remember me when you come into your kingdom.
V.   The rocks were split, the tombs were opened,
      and many bodies of the saints who slept were raised:
And the earth shook, and the thief from the cross cried out,
Lord, remember me when you come into your kingdom.

Lesson 9

But when Christ appeared as a high priest of the good things that are to come, then, through the greater and more perfect tent (not made with hands, that is, not of this creation), he entered once for all into the Holy Place, taking not the blood of goats and calves but his own blood, thus securing an eternal redemption. For if the sprinkling of defiled persons with the blood of goats and bulls and with the ashes of a heifer sanctifies for the purification of the flesh, how much more shall the blood of Christ, who through the eternal Spirit offered himself without blemish to God, purify your conscience from dead works to serve the living God. Therefore he is the mediator of a new covenant, so that those who are called may receive the promised eternal inheritance.

Responsory 9 *Sepulto Domino*

When the Lord was buried, they sealed the tomb,
rolling a great stone to the door of the tomb;
and they stationed soldiers to guard him.
V. The chief priests gathered before Pilate,
    and petitioned him:
And they stationed soldiers to guard him.

When this Responsory is sung rather than recited, repeat all that precedes the Verse:

When the Lord . . . to guard him.

Lauds

Antiphon 10

God did not spare his own Son, but delivered him up for us all.

Psalm 63, or *Psalm 63:1-8*

Antiphon 11

He was led like a lamb to the slaughter, and he opened not his mouth.

Psalm 90, or *Psalm 90:1-12*

Antiphon 12

They shall mourn for him as one mourns for an only child; for the Lord, who is without sin, is slain.

Psalm 143

Antiphon 13

From the gates of hell, O Lord, deliver my soul.

The Song of Hezekiah [Isaiah 38:10-20]

1 In my despair I said,
"In the noonday of my life I must depart; *
  my unspent years are summoned to the portals of death."

2 And I said,
"No more shall I see the Lord in the land of the living, *
  never more look on my kind among dwellers on earth.

3 My house is pulled down and I am uncovered, *
  as when a shepherd strikes his tent.

4 My life is rolled up like a bolt of cloth, *
  the threads cut off from the loom.

5 Between sunrise and sunset my life is brought to an end; *
  I cower and hope for the dawn.

6 Like a lion he has crushed all my bones; *
  like a swallow or thrush I utter plaintive cries;
  I mourn like a dove.

7 My weary eyes look up to you; *
   Lord, be my refuge in my affliction."

8 But what can I say? for he has spoken; *
   it is he who has done this.

9 Slow and halting are my steps all my days, *
   because of the bitterness of my spirit.

10 O Lord, I recounted all these things to you
   and you rescued me; *
      when entreated, you restored my life.

11 I know now that my bitterness was for my good, *
   for you held me back from the pit of destruction,
   you cast all my sins behind you.

12 The grave does not thank you nor death give you praise; *
   nor do those at the brink of the grave hang on your promises.

13 It is the living, O Lord,
   the living who give you thanks as I do this day; *
   and parents speak of your faithfulness to their children.

14 You, Lord, are my Savior; *
   I will praise you with stringed instruments
   all the days of my life, in the house of the Lord.

Ant. From the gates of hell, O Lord, deliver my soul.

Antiphon 14

O Death, I will be your death; O Grave, I will be your destruction.

Psalm 150

1 Praise God in his holy temple; *
   praise him in the firmament of his power.

2 Praise him for his mighty acts; *
     praise him for his excellent greatness.

3 Praise him with the blast of the ram's-horn; *
     praise him with lyre and harp.

4 Praise him with timbrel and dance; *
     praise him with strings and pipe.

5 Praise him with resounding cymbals; *
     praise him with loud-clanging cymbals.

6 Let everything that has breath *
     praise the Lord.

Ant. O Death, I will be your death;
         O Grave, I will be your destruction.

V. My flesh also shall rest in hope:
R. You will not let your holy One see corruption.

*All stand. During the singing of the following Canticle, the
candles at the Altar, and all other lights in the church (except the
one remaining at the top of the triangular candlestick), are
extinguished.*

Antiphon

Now the women sitting at the tomb made lamentation,
weeping for the Lord.

Canticle 16: Benedictus Dominus Deus Israel

*After the Canticle, during the repetition of the Antiphon, the
remaining candle is taken from the stand and hidden beneath or
behind the Altar, or in some other convenient place.*

Christus factus est

Christ for us became obedient unto death, even death on a cross; therefore God has highly exalted him and bestowed on him the Name which is above every name.

A brief silence is observed.

The following Psalm is then said quietly. If it is sung, it is customary to monotone alternate verses.

Psalm 51

The Officiant says the Collect without chant, and without the usual conclusion.

Almighty God, we pray you graciously to behold this your family, for whom our Lord Jesus Christ was willing to be betrayed, and given into the hands of sinners, and to suffer death upon the cross.

Nothing further is said; but a noise is made, and the remaining candle is brought from its hiding place and replaced on the stand.

By its light the ministers and people depart in silence.

Additional Directions

This book provides for the full ancient form of the service: Matins, subdivided into three Nocturns, and Lauds. If desired, the service may be shortened somewhat by using the shorter form indicated for certain of the Psalms. The first two responsories of each Nocturn may also be omitted.

In preparation for the service, a large triangular candlestick with fifteen candles is placed at the liturgical south side of the sanctuary. One candle is extinguished at the end of each Psalm, and at the end of the Song of Hezekiah. Finally, during the singing of the canticle Benedictus, the candles at the Altar, and all other lights (except the one at the top of the triangular stand), are extinguished.

There should be no musical prelude or postlude at this service, nor should a processional cross or torches be carried, or hymns sung, or sermons preached.

The ministers, servers, and choir vest in the manner customary for choir offices. The officiant may wear a tippet over the surplice.

The appointed antiphons are sung or recited in full before and after each Psalm. The Psalms themselves are sung or recited antiphonally. Gloria Patri is not used at this service.

Each group of lessons is announced only at the beginning, as indicated in the text. The usual concluding formula is omitted.

The successive letters of the Hebrew alphabet, prefixed to the verses of the readings from Lamentations, are an integral part of the traditional chant, and should not be omitted when these lessons are sung. (In the Hebrew original, each verse begins with the letter indicated.)

If the responsories after the lessons are recited rather than sung, the congregation reads the parts in italics. In musical settings the responsories may be sung in full by the choir or by all; the verse [V.] may be sung by a solo voice. The repetition of the first part of the text in Responsories 3, 6, and 9 is intended for use in musical settings only.

If a much shorter form of the service is desired, Nocturns 2 and 3 and the second or third Psalm of Lauds (Psalm 90 or 143) may be omitted. In this case two candles are extinguished after each Psalm. Alternatively, Nocturns 2 and 3 and two of the Lauds' Psalms may be omitted, and a seven-branched candlestick used.

On Maundy Thursday

At the Foot-Washing

If it is desired to introduce the ceremony of foot-washing by a brief address, the following may be used:

Fellow servants of our Lord Jesus Christ: On the night before his death, Jesus set an example for his disciples by washing their feet, an act of humble service. He taught that strength and growth in the life of the Kingdom of God come not by power, authority, or even miracle, but by such lowly service. We all need to remember his example, but none stand more in need of this reminder than those whom the Lord has called to the ordained ministry.

Therefore, I invite you [who have been appointed as representatives of the congregation and] who share in the royal priesthood of Christ, to come forward, that I may recall whose servant I am by following the example of my Master. But come remembering his admonition that what will be done for you is also to be done by you to others, for "a servant is not greater than his master, nor is one who is sent greater than the one who sent him. If you know these things, blessed are you if you do them."

On Reserving the Sacrament

When the Sacrament is to be reserved for administration on Good Friday, it should be kept in a separate chapel or other place apart from the main sanctuary of the church, in order that on Good Friday the attention of the congregation may be on the bare main Altar.

On the Stripping of the Altar

If the custom of stripping the Altar is observed as a public ceremony, it takes place after the Maundy Thursday liturgy. It may be done in silence; or it may be accompanied by the recitation of Psalm 22, which is said without Gloria Patri. The following antiphon may be said before and after the Psalm.

They divide my garments among them; they cast lots for my clothing.

Agapé for Maundy Thursday

The celebration of festal meals is not appropriate during Holy Week. In Christian tradition such festivities take place only after the Lenten fast has been completed by the celebration of the Great Vigil – which is the Passover Feast of Christians – and the reception of Easter Communion.

If it is desired to share a meal after the Maundy Thursday Eucharist, the following order may be observed.

A meatless meal is to be preferred. The setting should be austere and the foods sparse and simple. Appropriate foods include soup, cheese, olives, dried fruit, bread, and wine. It is suitable that the bread and wine for the meal be brought to the Altar at the time of the Offertory (along with special offerings for the hungry), and after the service taken to the room where the meal is to take place.

The following blessings are recited by the Celebrant at the beginning of the meal, all standing.

Over Wine

Blessed are you, O Lord our God, King of the universe. You create the fruit of the vine; and on this night you have refreshed us with the cup of salvation in the Blood of your Son Jesus Christ. Glory to you for ever and ever. *Amen.*

Over Bread

Blessed are you, O Lord our God, King of the universe. You bring forth bread from the earth; and on this night you have given us the bread of life in the Body of your Son Jesus Christ. As grain scattered upon the earth is gathered into one loaf, so gather your Church in every place into the kingdom of your Son. To you be glory and power for ever and ever. *Amen.*

Over the Other Foods

Blessed are you, O Lord our God, King of the universe. You have blessed the earth to bring forth food to satisfy our hunger. Let this food strengthen us in the fast that is before us, that following our Savior in the way of the cross, we may come to the joy of his resurrection. For yours is the kingdom and the power and the glory, now and for ever. *Amen.*

During the meal or toward its close, a person appointed reads the seventeenth chapter of the Gospel according to John.

The agapé concludes with a psalm, such as Psalm 69:1-23, or with a song, or with a prayer, or with a blessing or dismissal.

If an agapé is held, the ceremony of stripping the Altar is deferred until after the meal.

The form for the agapé given above may also be used in private homes on this night.

Blessings Over Food at Easter

These blessings are appropriate for use by households at the principal meal on Easter Day. They may be used at a parish meal following the Easter Vigil. They may also be used over foods brought to the church for blessing.

Over Wine

Blessed are you, O Lord our God, creator of the fruit of the vine: Grant that we who share this wine, which gladdens our hearts, may share for ever the new life of the true Vine, your Son Jesus Christ our Lord. *Amen.*

Over Bread

Blessed are you, O Lord our God; you bring forth bread from the earth and make the risen Lord to be for us the Bread of life: Grant that we who daily seek the bread which sustains our bodies may also hunger for the food of everlasting life, Jesus Christ our Lord. *Amen.*

Over Lamb

Stir up our memory, O Lord, as we eat this Easter lamb that, remembering Israel of old, who in obedience to your command ate the Paschal lamb and was delivered from the bondage of slavery, we, your new Israel, may rejoice in the resurrection of Jesus Christ, the true Lamb who has delivered us from the bondage of sin and death, and who lives and reigns for ever and ever. *Amen.*

Over Eggs

O Lord our God, in celebration of the Paschal feast we have prepared these eggs from your creation: Grant that they may be to us a sign of the new life and immortality promised to those who follow your Son, Jesus Christ our Lord. *Amen.*

Over Other Foods

Blessed are you, O Lord our God; you have given us the risen Savior to be the Shepherd of your people: Lead us, by him, to springs of living waters, and feed us with the food that endures to eternal life; where with you, O Father, and with the Holy Spirit, he lives and reigns, one God, for ever and ever. *Amen.*

Blessing in Homes at Easter

Where it is customary to invite the parish priest to the homes of parishioners during the Fifty Days of Easter, this blessing may be used.

The Celebrant begins with the following or some other greeting

Peace be to this house, and to all who dwell in it.

Psalm 114 is then sung or said with one of the following antiphons:

Alleluia. The Lord is risen indeed: Come let us adore him. Alleluia.

or this

I saw water proceeding out of the temple; from the right side it flowed, alleluia; and all those to whom that water came shall be saved, and shall say, alleluia, alleluia.

When Israel came out of Egypt, *
  the house of Jacob from a people of strange speech,
Judah became God's sanctuary *
  and Israel his dominion.
The sea beheld it and fled; *
  Jordan turned and went back.
The mountains skipped like rams, *
  and the little hills like young sheep.

What ailed you, O sea, that you fled? *
    O Jordan, that you turned back?
You mountains, that you skipped like rams? *
    you little hills like young sheep?
Tremble, O earth, at the presence of the Lord, *
    at the presence of the God of Jacob,
Who turned the hard rock into a pool of water *
    and flint-stone into a flowing spring.
Glory to the Father, and to the Son, and to the Holy Spirit: *
    as it was in the beginning, is now, and will be for ever. Amen.

The antiphon is then repeated.

Another psalm, such as Psalm 118, may be used in place of Psalm 114,
or a canticle may be substituted. Suitable canticles are Christ our
Passover, the Song of Moses, and the Song to the Lamb.

Celebrant The Lord be with you.
People   And also with you.
Celebrant Let us pray.

The Celebrant says one of the following Collects, or some other Collect
of the Easter Season.

Grant, we pray, Almighty God, that we who celebrate with
awe the Paschal feast may be found worthy to attain to
everlasting joys; through Jesus Christ our Lord, who lives
and reigns with you and the Holy Spirit, one God, now and
for ever. *Amen.*

or this

Almighty and everlasting God, who in the Paschal mystery
established the new covenant of reconciliation: Grant that
all who have been reborn into the fellowship of Christ's
Body may show forth in their lives what they profess by their

faith; through Jesus Christ our Lord, who lives and reigns with you and the Holy Spirit, one God, for ever and ever. *Amen.*

The Celebrant then says this prayer

Visit, O blessed Lord, this home with the gladness of your presence. Bless *all* who *live* here with the gift of your love; and grant that *they* may manifest your love [to each other and] to all whose lives *they touch*. May *they* grow in grace and in the knowledge and love of you; guide, comfort, and strengthen *them*; and preserve *them* in peace, O Jesus Christ, now and for ever. *Amen.*

The Celebrant may say one of the two following blessings:

May God the Father, who by Baptism adopts us as his children, grant you grace. *Amen.*

May God the Son, who sanctified a home at Nazareth, fill you with love. *Amen.*

May God the Holy Spirit, who has made the Church one family, keep you in peace. *Amen.*

or this

May Almighty God, who has redeemed us and made us his children through the resurrection of his Son our Lord, bestow upon you the riches of his blessing. *Amen.*

May God, who through the water of baptism has raised us from sin into newness of life, make you holy and worthy to be united with Christ for ever. *Amen.*

May God, who has brought us out of bondage to sin into true and lasting freedom in the Redeemer, bring you to your eternal inheritance. *Amen.*

And the blessing of God Almighty, the Father, the Son, and the Holy Spirit, be upon you and remain with you for ever. *Amen.*

The Peace may then be exchanged.

Rogation Procession

The Rogation Days are traditionally observed on the Monday, Tuesday, and Wednesday before Ascension Day. They may, however, be observed on other days, depending on local conditions and the convenience of the congregation.

Anciently, the observance consisted of an outdoor procession which culminated in a special celebration of the Eucharist. In more recent centuries, the procession has frequently taken place on a Sunday afternoon, apart from the Eucharist.

If the Rogation Procession is held on a Sunday or Principal Feast, it should take place apart from or following the Proper Eucharist of the Day. Under these conditions the procession concludes with a suitable prayer and a blessing.

Hymns, psalms, canticles, and anthems are sung during the procession. The following are appropriate:

Canticle 1 or 12 (Benedicite)
Psalm 103 (Refrain: "Bless the Lord, O my soul")
Psalm 104 (Refrain: "Hallelujah").

At suitable places the procession may halt for appropriate Bible readings and prayers.

In addition to the readings listed on page 930 of the Prayer Book, any of the following passages are appropriate:

Genesis 8:13-23	Ezekiel 34:25-31
Leviticus 26:1-13(14-20)	James 4:7-11
Deuteronomy 8:1-10(11-20)	Matthew 6:25-34
Hosea 2:18-23	John 12:23-26

Suitable prayers include the following: Prayers 1, 29, 34, 38, 40-44, and Thanksgivings 1, 8, 9 from the section "Prayers and Thanksgivings" in the Prayer Book. Also, the following

Almighty and everlasting God, Creator of all things and giver of all life, let your blessing be upon this (seed, livestock, plough, forest, _____) and grant that *it* may serve to your glory and the welfare of your people; through Jesus Christ our Lord. *Amen.*

Customarily, the Great Litany is begun as the procession enters the church. The following petitions may be inserted following the third petition on page 151 of the Prayer Book:

That it may please thee to grant favorable weather, temperate rain, and fruitful seasons, that there may be food and drink for all thy creatures,
We beseech thee to hear us, good Lord.

That it may please thee to bless the lands and waters, and all who work upon them to bring forth food and all things needful for thy people,
We beseech thee to hear us, good Lord.

That it may please thee to look with favor upon all who care for the earth, the water, and the air, that the riches of thy creation may abound from age to age,
We beseech thee to hear us, good Lord.

At the conclusion of the Litany, after the Kyries, the Eucharist begins with the Salutation and one of the Proper Collects for Rogation Days.

*If the procession cannot take place out of doors, the service may begin
with the Great Litany, which may be sung in procession in the church.*

*If the Liturgy does not begin with the Great Litany, it is suggested that
Form V be used for the Prayers of the People, and that the following
petitions be added after the eighth petition on page 390:*

For favorable weather, temperate rains, and fruitful seasons,
that there may be food and drink for all your creatures, we
pray to you, O Lord.

For your blessing upon the lands and waters, and all who
work upon them to bring forth food and all things needful
for your people, we pray to you, O Lord.

For all who care for the earth, the water, and the air, that the
riches of your creation may abound from age to age, we pray
to you, O Lord.

Vigil for the
Eve of All Saints' Day

or the Sunday after All Saints' Day

*When a Baptismal Vigil of All Saints is observed, it begins with the
Service of Light, page 109 of the Prayer Book (substituting, if desired,
the Gloria in excelsis for the Phos hilaron), and continues with the
Salutation and Collect of the Day. Three or more Lessons are read before
the Gospel, each followed by a period of silence and a Psalm, Canticle,
or hymn. Holy Baptism or Confirmation (beginning with the
Presentation of the Candidates), or the Renewal of Baptismal Vows,
Prayer Book page 292, follows the Sermon.*

The Call of Abraham
Genesis 12:1-8

Psalm 113

Daniel Delivered from the Lions' Den
Daniel 6: (1-15) 16-23

Canticle 2 or 13

The Testament and Death of Mattathias
1 Maccabees 2:49-64

Psalm 1

The Martyrdom of the Seven Brothers
2 Maccabees 6:1-2; 7:1-23

Psalm 111

The Eulogy of the Ancestors *
Ecclesiasticus 44:1-10, 13-14

Psalm 116

Surrounded by a Great Cloud of Witnesses †
Hebrews 11:32 (33-38) 39—12:2

Psalm 149*

The Reward of the Saints *
Revelation 7:2-4, 9-17

The Beatitudes *
Matthew 5:1-12

or **"I will give you rest"**
    Matthew 11:27-30

or **The Resurrection and the Great Commission°**
    Matthew 28:1-10, 16-20

* Proper Readings and Psalm for the Eucharist of All Saints.
† Appointed also for Morning Prayer on All Saints' Day.
° On Saturday evening only.

Service for All Hallows' Eve

This service may be used on the evening of October 31, known as All Hallows' Eve. Suitable festivities and entertainments may take place before or after this service, and a visit may be made to a cemetery or burial place.

The rite begins with the Service of Light, page 109 of the Prayer Book, using the Prayer for Light appointed for Festivals of Saints.

After the Phos hilaron, two or more of the following lessons are read, each followed by a Psalm, Canticle, or hymn, and a Prayer.

The Witch of Endor
1 Samuel 28:3-25
(It is appropriate that this lesson be read by a narrator, and by other readers for Saul, the witch, and Samuel.)

Psalm 130

Let us pray.   *(Silence)*

Almighty and everliving God, you have made all things in your wisdom and established the boundaries of life and death: Grant that we may obey your voice in this world, and in the world to come may enjoy that rest and peace which you have appointed for your people; through Jesus Christ who is Resurrection and Life, and who lives and reigns for ever and ever. *Amen.*

The Vision of Eliphaz the Temanite
Job 4:12-21

Psalm 13, *or* Psalm 108:1-6

Let us pray. *(Silence)*

You, O Lord, have made us from the dust of the earth and to dust our bodies shall return; yet you have also breathed your Spirit upon us and called us to new life in you: Have mercy upon us, now and at the hour of our death; through Jesus Christ, our mediator and advocate. *Amen.*

The Valley of Dry Bones
Ezekiel 37:1-14

Psalm 143:1-11

Let us pray. *(Silence)*

O God, you have called your people to your service from age to age. Do not give us over to death, but raise us up to serve you, to praise you, and to glorify your holy Name; through Jesus Christ our Lord. *Amen.*

The War in Heaven
Revelation 12:(1-6) 7-12

Psalm 103:17-22, *or* Canticle 1 (parts I & IV) *or* Canticle 12 (Invocation, Part III, Doxology)

Let us pray. *(Silence)*

O most merciful and mighty God, your son Jesus Christ was born of the Blessed Virgin Mary to bring us salvation and to establish your kingdom on earth: Grant that Michael and all your angels may defend your people against Satan and every evil foe, and that at the last we may come to that heavenly country where your saints for ever sing your praise; through Jesus Christ our Lord. *Amen.*

A homily, sermon, or instruction may follow the Readings.

The service then concludes with the singing of Te Deum laudamus or some other song of praise, the Lord's Prayer, the Collect of All Saints' Day, and a blessing or dismissal.

Pastoral Services

Welcoming New People
To a Congregation

If it is desired to welcome new people to the congregation publicly, it is suitable that they be introduced in the following manner.

Immediately before the Peace, the persons are asked to come forward, and are introduced briefly, preferably by a member of the congregation.

The celebrant then begins the exchange of the Peace, in the course of which those who have been introduced are greeted personally by the celebrant and members of the congregation as convenient.

When Members
Leave a Congregation

When persons leave a congregation, it is suitable that, on their last Sunday, the fact be mentioned before the Prayers of the People, and that they be prayed for by name in those Prayers.

They are greeted personally by the celebrant and lay officials of the congregation at the time of the Peace, or at the end of the service.

Concerning the Catechumenate

The systematic instruction and formation of its catechumens is a solemn responsibility of the Christian community. Traditionally, the preparation of catechumens is a responsibility of the bishop, which is shared with the presbyters, deacons, and appointed lay catechists of the diocese.

The catechumenate is a period of training and instruction in Christian understandings about God, human relationships, and the meaning of life, which culminates in the reception of the Sacraments of Christian Initiation. It is marked by three stages.

Stage 1. The Pre-catechumenal Period. To this stage belong inquirers' classes with sufficient preparation to enable persons to determine that they wish to become Christians. It is a time during which those who have been initially attracted to the Christian community are guided to examine and test their motives, in order that they may freely commit themselves to pursue a disciplined exploration of the implications of Christian living.

Stage 2. The Catechumenate. Entry into the catechumenate is by a public liturgical act (which may take place for individuals or groups at any time) at the principal Sunday liturgy. Normatively, the act includes signing with the cross. To this stage belong regular association with the worshiping community, the practice of life in accordance with the Gospel (including service to the poor and neglected), encouragement and instruction in the life of prayer, and basic instruction in the history of salvation as revealed in the Holy Scriptures of the Old and New Testaments. This stage will vary in length according to the needs of the individual. For those persons who, although unbaptized, already possess an understanding and appreciation of the Christian religion, it might be relatively short.

Each person to be admitted a catechumen is presented by a sponsor who normally accompanies the catechumen through the process of candidacy and serves as sponsor at Holy Baptism.

Admission to the catechumenate is an appropriate time to determine the name by which one desires to be known in the Christian community. This may be one's given name, a new name legally changed, or an additional name of Christian significance.

From the time of admission, a catechumen is regarded as a part of the Christian community. For example, a person who dies during the catechumenate receives a Christian burial.

Stage 3. Candidacy for Baptism. To this stage belong a series of liturgical acts leading up to baptism. These ordinarily take place on a series of Sundays preceding one of the stated days for baptism, and involve public prayer for the candidates, who are present at the services as a group, accompanied by their sponsors. When the Sacrament of Holy Baptism is administered at Easter, enrollment as a candidate normally takes place at the beginning of Lent; when baptisms are planned for the Feast of the Baptism of Our Lord, the enrollment takes place at the beginning of Advent.

In addition to these public acts, this stage involves the private disciplines of fasting, examination of conscience, and prayer, in order that the candidates will be spiritually and emotionally ready for baptism. It is appropriate that, in accordance with ancient custom, the sponsors support their candidates by joining them in prayer and fasting.

A fourth period immediately follows the administration of Holy Baptism. In the case of persons baptized at the Great Vigil, it extends over the Fifty Days of Easter. This period is devoted to such activities, formal and informal, as will assist the newly baptized to experience the fullness of the corporate life of the Church and to gain a deeper understanding of the meaning of the Sacraments.

The bishop, the bishop's representative, or the rector (or priest-in-charge) of the congregation should preside at the rites of Admission and Enrollment.

It should be noted that the rites and prayers which follow are appropriate for use only with persons preparing for baptism. Validly baptized Christians present at instruction classes to deepen their understanding of the faith, including members of other Christian bodies preparing to be received into the Episcopal Church, are under no circumstances to be considered catechumens. The same is true of persons preparing to re-affirm their baptismal vows after having abandoned the practice of the Christian religion, since "The bond which God establishes in Baptism is indissoluble" (Prayer Book, page 298).

Preparation of Adults for Holy Baptism

Admission of Catechumens

The admission of catechumens may take place at any time of the year, within a principal Sunday liturgy.

After the sermon (or after the Creed) the Celebrant invites those to be admitted as catechumens to come forward with their sponsors.

The Celebrant then asks the following question of those to be admitted. If desired, the question may be asked of each person individually.

What do you seek?

Answer   Life in Christ.

The Celebrant then says,

Jesus said, "The first commandment is this: Hear, O Israel: The Lord our God is the only Lord. Love the Lord your God with all your heart, with all your soul, and with all your strength. The second is this: Love your neighbor as yourself. There is no other commandment greater than these." Do you accept these commandments?

Answer   I do.

Celebrant Do you promise to be regular in attending the worship of God and in receiving instruction?

Answer I do.

Celebrant Will you open your ears to hear the Word of God and your heart and mind to receive the Lord Jesus?

Answer I will, with God's help.

The Celebrant then addresses the sponsors

Will you who sponsor *these persons* support *them* by prayer and example and help *them* to grow in the knowledge and love of God?

Sponsors I will.

Those to be admitted kneel. The sponsors remain standing, and place a hand upon the shoulder of the one they are sponsoring, while the Celebrant extends a hand toward them and says

May Almighty God, our heavenly Father, who has put the desire into your *hearts* to seek the grace of our Lord Jesus Christ, grant you the power of the Holy Spirit to persevere in this intention and to grow in faith and understanding.

People Amen.

Each of those to be admitted is presented by name to the Celebrant, who, with the thumb, marks a cross on the forehead of each, saying

N., receive the sign of the Cross on your forehead and in your heart, in the Name of the Father, and of the Son, and of the Holy Spirit.

People Amen.

The Sponsors also mark a cross on the foreheads of their catechumens.

The catechumens and sponsors then return to their places.

The Liturgy continues with (the Creed and) the Prayers of the People, in the course of which prayer is offered for the new catechumens by name.

If any of the catechumens, after consultation with the celebrant, wishes to renounce a former way of worship, an appropriately worded renunciation may be included immediately following the first question and answer.

During the Catechumenate

During this period, and continuing through the period of Candidacy, formal instruction is given to the catechumens. At the conclusion of each session, a period of silence is observed, during which the catechumens pray for themselves and one another. Sponsors and other baptized persons present offer their prayers for the catechumens. The instructor then says one or two of the following or some other suitable prayers, and concludes by laying a hand individually on the head of each catechumen in silence. It is traditional that this act be performed by the instructor, whether bishop, priest, deacon, or lay catechist.

1

O God, the creator and savior of all flesh, look with mercy on your *children* whom you call to yourself in love. Cleanse *their hearts* and guard *them* as *they prepare* to receive your Sacraments that, led by your Holy Spirit, *they* may be united with your Son, and enter into the inheritance of your sons and daughters; through Jesus Christ our Lord. *Amen.*

2

O God of truth, of beauty, and of goodness, we give you
thanks that from the beginning of creation you have revealed
yourself in the things that you have made; and that in every
nation, culture, and language there have been those who,
seeing your works, have worshiped you and sought to do
your will. Accept our prayers for *these* your *servants* whom
you have called to know and love you as you have been
perfectly revealed in your Son Jesus Christ our Redeemer, and
bring *them* with joy to new birth in the waters of Baptism;
through Jesus Christ our Lord. *Amen.*

3

O God of righteousness and truth, you inaugurated your
victory over the forces of deceit and sin by the Advent of
your Son: Give to *these catechumens* a growing
understanding of the truth as it is in Jesus; and grant that
they, being cleansed from sin and born again in the waters of
Baptism, may glorify with us the greatness of your Name;
through Jesus Christ our Lord. *Amen.*

4

O God, in your pity you looked upon a fallen world, and
sent your only Son among us to vanquish the powers of
wickedness. Deliver *these* your *servants* from slavery to sin
and evil. Purify *their* desires and thoughts with the light of
your Holy Spirit. Nourish *them* with your holy Word,
strengthen *them* in faith, and confirm *them* in good works;
through Jesus Christ our Lord. *Amen.*

5

Look down in mercy, Lord, upon *these catechumens* now
being taught in your holy Word. Open *their* ears to hear and

their hearts to obey. Bring to *their minds their* past sins, committed against you and against *their* neighbors, that *they* may truly repent of them. And in your mercy preserve *them* in *their* resolve to seek your kingdom and your righteousness; through Jesus Christ our Lord. *Amen.*

6

Drive out of *these catechumens,* Lord God, every trace of wickedness. Protect *them* from the Evil One. Bring *them* to the saving waters of baptism, and make *them* yours for ever; through Jesus Christ our Lord. *Amen.*

7

Lord Jesus Christ, loving Redeemer of all, you alone have the power to save. At your Name every knee shall bow, whether in heaven, on earth, or under the earth. We pray to you for *these catechumens* who *seek* to serve you, the one true God. Send your light into *their hearts*, protect *them* from the hatred of the Evil One, heal in *them* the wounds of sin, and strengthen *them* against temptation. Give *them* a love of your commandments, and courage to live always by your Gospel, and so prepare *them* to receive your Spirit; you who live and reign for ever and ever. *Amen.*

8

Most merciful God, behold and sustain *these catechumens* who *seek* to know you more fully: Free *them* from the grasp of Satan, and make *them* bold to renounce all sinful desires that entice *them* from loving you; that, coming in faith to the Sacrament of Baptism, *they* may commit *themselves* to you, receive the seal of the Holy Spirit, and share with us in the eternal priesthood of Jesus Christ our Lord. *Amen.*

9

Lord God, unfailing light and source of light, by the death and resurrection of your Christ you have cast out hatred and deceit, and poured upon the human family the light of truth and love: Look upon *these catechumens* whom you have called to enter your covenant, free *them* from the power of the Prince of darkness, and number *them* among the children of promise; through Jesus Christ our Lord. *Amen.*

10

Stir up, O Lord, the *wills* of *these catechumens,* and assist *them* by your grace, that *they* may bring forth plenteously the fruit of good works, and receive from you a rich reward; through Jesus Christ our Lord. *Amen.*

Enrollment of Candidates for Baptism

The enrollment of candidates for Baptism at the Great Vigil of Easter normally takes place on the First Sunday in Lent. For those preparing for Baptism on the Feast of our Lord's Baptism, it takes place on the First Sunday of Advent.

The large book in which the names of the candidates for Baptism are to be written is placed where it can easily be seen and used.

After the Creed, the catechumens to be enrolled are invited to come forward with their sponsors.

A Catechist, or other lay representative of the congregation, presents them to the bishop or priest with the following or similar words

I present to you *these catechumens* who *have* been strengthened by God's grace and supported by the example and prayers of this congregation, and I ask that *they* be enrolled as *candidates* for Holy Baptism.

The Celebrant asks the sponsors

Have they been regular in attending the worship of God and in receiving instruction?

Sponsors   They have. (*He* has.)

Celebrant   *Are they* seeking by prayer, study, and example to pattern *their lives* in accordance with the Gospel?
Sponsors   They are. (*He* is.)

The Celebrant asks the sponsors and congregation

As God is your witness, do you approve the enrolling of *these catechumens* as *candidates* for Holy Baptism?

Answer   We do.

The Celebrant addresses the catechumens

Do you desire to be baptized?

Catechumens   I do.

The Celebrant then says

In the Name of God, and with the consent of this congregation, I accept you as *candidates* for Holy Baptism, and direct that your *names* be written in this book. God grant that *they* may also be written in the Book of Life.

The candidates then publicly write their names in the book; or, if necessary, someone else may write the names. Each name is said aloud at the time of writing. The sponsors may also sign the book.

The candidates remain together at the front of the church while the Deacon, or other person appointed, leads the following litany:

In peace let us pray to the Lord, saying "Lord, have mercy."

For *these catechumens*, that *they* may remember this day on which *they were* chosen, and remain for ever grateful for this heavenly blessing, let us pray to the Lord.
Lord, have mercy.

That *they* may use this Lenten season wisely, joining with us in acts of self-denial and in performing works of mercy, let us pray to the Lord.
Lord, have mercy.

For *their* teachers, that they may make known to those whom they teach the riches of the Word of God, let us pray to the Lord.
Lord, have mercy.

For *their* sponsor(s), that in *their* private *lives* and public actions *they* may show to *these candidates* a pattern of life in accordance with the Gospel, let us pray to the Lord.
Lord, have mercy.

For *their families* and friends, that they may place no obstacles in the way of *these candidates*, but rather assist *them* to follow the promptings of the Spirit, let us pray to the Lord.
Lord, have mercy.

For this congregation, that [during this Lenten season] it may abound in love and persevere in prayer, let us pray to the Lord.
Lord, have mercy.

For our Bishop, and for all the clergy and people, let us pray to the Lord.
Lord, have mercy.

For our President, for the leaders of the nations, and for all in authority, let us pray to the Lord.
Lord, have mercy.

For the sick and the sorrowful, and for those in any need or trouble, let us pray to the Lord.
Lord, have mercy.

For _____, let us pray to the Lord.
Lord, have mercy.

For all who have died in the hope of the resurrection, and for all the departed, let us pray to the Lord.
Lord, have mercy.

In the communion of [_____ and of all the] saints, let us commend ourselves, and one another, and all our life, to Christ our God.
To you, O Lord our God.

Silence

The Celebrant says the following prayer with hands extended over the candidates

Immortal God, Lord Jesus Christ, the protector of all who come to you, the life of those who believe, and the resurrection of the dead: We call upon you for *these* your *servants* who *desire* the grace of spiritual rebirth in the Sacrament of Holy Baptism. Accept *them,* Lord Christ, as you promised when you said, "Ask, and it will be given you; seek, and you will find; knock, and it will be opened to you." Give now, we pray, to those who ask, let those who seek find, open the gate to those who knock; that *these* your *servants* may receive the everlasting benediction of your heavenly washing, and come to that promised kingdom which you have prepared, and where you live and reign for ever and ever. *Amen.*

The candidates then return to their places and the Liturgy continues with the Confession of Sin or with the Peace.

During Candidacy

On the Sundays preceding their baptism, the candidates attend public worship with their sponsors, and both the candidates and sponsors are prayed for by name in the Prayers of the People. (When Eucharistic Prayer D is used, however, it is appropriate that the names be inserted at the place provided in that prayer.)

In addition, the following prayers and blessings may be used immediately before the Prayers of the People, especially on the Third, Fourth, and Fifth Sundays in Lent (or, the Second, Third, and Fourth Sundays of Advent). When these prayers are used, the candidates and sponsors are called forward. The candidates kneel or bow their heads. The sponsors each place a hand upon the shoulder of their candidate.

The Celebrant then calls the people to prayer in these or similar words

Let us pray in silence, dearly beloved, for *these candidates* who *are* preparing to receive the illumination of the Holy Spirit in the Sacrament of Baptism.

All pray in silence.

The Celebrant says one of the following prayers:

Lord God, in the beginning of creation you called forth light to dispel the darkness that lay upon the face of the deep: Deliver *these* your *servants* from the powers of evil and illumine *them* with the light of your presence, that with open eyes and glad hearts *they* may worship you and serve you, now and for ever; through Jesus Christ our Lord. *Amen.*

or this

Lord Christ, true Light who enlightens every one: Shine, we pray, in the *hearts* of *these candidates*, that *they* may clearly see the way that leads to life eternal, and may follow it without stumbling; for you yourself are the Way, O Christ, as you are the Truth and the Life; and you live and reign for ever and ever. *Amen.*

or this

Come, O Holy Spirit, come; come as the wind and cleanse; come as the fire and burn; convict, convert, and consecrate the minds and hearts of *these* your *servants*, to *their* great good and to your great glory; who with the Father and the Son are one God, now and for ever. *Amen.*

The Celebrant lays a hand on the head of each candidate in silence.

The Celebrant then adds one of the following blessings:

May Almighty God bestow upon you the blessing of his mercy, and give you an understanding of the wisdom that leads to salvation; through Christ our Lord. *Amen.*

or this

May Almighty God keep your steps from wandering from the way of truth, and cause you to walk in the paths of peace and love; through Christ our Lord. *Amen.*

or this

May Almighty God nourish you with true knowledge of the catholic faith, and grant you to persevere in every good work; through Christ our Lord. *Amen.*

The candidates and sponsors return to their places and the Liturgy continues.

A Vigil on the Eve of Baptism

When it is desired to celebrate a vigil on the eve of the Bishop's Visitation or other occasion in preparation for the administration of baptism at a principal Sunday morning service, the following order may be used.

The Vigil begins with the Service of Light, Prayer Book page 109, and continues, after the Phos hilaron, with the Salutation and Collect. Three or more of the appointed Lessons are read before the Gospel, each followed by a period of silence and a Psalm, Canticle, or hymn.

If the Vigil takes place on the eve of Pentecost, All Saints' Day or the Sunday following, or the Feast of the Baptism of our Lord, the Proper Collect, Psalms, and Lessons appointed for those vigils are used. On other occasions any appropriate Collect may be selected, and the Readings chosen from among the following:

The Story of the Flood
Genesis (7:1-5, 11-18); 8:6-18; 9:8-13

Psalm 25:3-9,   *or*   Psalm 46

The Story of the Covenant
Exodus 19:1-9a, 16-20a; 20:18-20

Canticle 2 or 13

Salvation Offered Freely to All
Isaiah 55:1-11

Canticle 9

A New Heart and a New Spirit
Ezekiel 36:24-28

Psalm 42

The Valley of Dry Bones
Ezekiel 37:1-14

Psalm 30   *or*   Psalm 143

Baptized into his Death
Romans 6:3-5

or   **We are Children of God**
      Romans 8:14-17

or   **Now is the Day of Salvation**
      2 Corinthians 5:17-20

The Baptism of Jesus
Mark 1:1-6

or   **You Must be Born Again**
      John 3:1-6

or   **The Resurrection and the Great Commission**
      Matthew 28:1-10, 16-20

After the Gospel (and homily) the candidates and their sponsors are called forward. The candidates kneel or bow their heads. The Sponsors each place a hand upon the shoulder of their candidate. The Celebrant then lays a hand on the head of each candidate in silence.

The Celebrant then says one of the following forms of prayer, after which a hymn may be sung. The service then concludes with a blessing or dismissal, or both.

Form 1

Holy Trinity, one God, be present at the font *tomorrow* for the sake of *these* your *servants*. Amen.

At the invocation of your great Name, let the life-giving Spirit sanctify the waters. *Amen.*

There let the old Adam be buried, and the new be raised up. *Amen.*

There let the power of evil be broken, and the power of the Spirit be revealed. *Amen.*

Strip from *these* your *servants* the soiled and tattered garb of sin, and clothe *them* with the shining robe of immortality. *Amen.*

Help *them* to know that all who are baptized into Christ have put on Christ. *Amen.*

Let *them* and all who, at the font, renounce Satan and every evil power, receive strength to overcome temptation. *Amen.*

Whoever there confesses you as Lord, acknowledge, O Lord, in your kingdom. *Amen.*

Lead them with joy from the font to the altar, and prepare for them a place at your heavenly banquet. *Amen.*

Banish from them the fear of death, and give them a sure faith in your promises. *Amen.*

Teach them to deny themselves for the sake of your Gospel, that they may never lose you, their everlasting treasure. *Amen.*

Let every one who is dedicated to you through the ministry of your holy Church be bound to you for ever, and everlastingly rewarded. *Amen.*

Grant this in your mercy, O God, for you are the ruler over all, and you live and are blessed for evermore. *Amen.*

Form 2

Lord Jesus Christ, you desire that everyone who follows you shall be born again by water and the Spirit:

Remember your *servants* [*N.N.*] who tomorrow are to be baptized in your Name.

By *their names* Lord:

Grant that you will know *them*, and call *them* to a life of service. *Amen.*

Grant that *they* may become the *persons* you created *them* to be. *Amen.*

Grant that *they* may be written for ever in your Book of Life. *Amen.*

Through the water of *their* baptism, Lord:

Grant that *they* may be united with you in your death. *Amen.*

Grant that *they* may receive forgiveness for all *their* sins. *Amen.*

Grant that *they* may have power to endure, and strength to have victory in the battle of life. *Amen.*

As *members* of your Church, Lord:

Grant that *they* may rise to a new life in the fellowship of those who love you. *Amen.*

Grant that *they* may suffer when another suffers, and when another rejoices, rejoice. *Amen.*

Grant that *they* may be your faithful *soldiers* and *servants* until *their* life's end. *Amen.*

Through the abiding presence of your Spirit, Lord:

Grant that *they* may lead the rest of *their lives* according to this beginning. *Amen.*

Grant that when *they pass* through the dark waters of death, you will be with *them*. *Amen.*

Grant that *they* may inherit the kingdom of glory prepared for *them* from the foundation of the world. *Amen.*

To you, Lord Christ, with the Father and the Holy Spirit, be honor and glory in the Church, now and for ever. *Amen.*

Celebration for a Home

The celebrant, members of the household, and friends assemble in the living room of the home (in which a table has been prepared for the Holy Communion).

The Celebrant greets the people.

The service may begin with the following or some other appropriate Collect, the Celebrant first saying

> The Lord be with you.
People   And also with you.
Celebrant Let us pray.

Almighty and everlasting God, grant to this home [*PLACE*] the grace of your presence, that you may be known to be the inhabitant of this dwelling, and the defender of this [*SERVICE*] household; through Jesus Christ our Lord, who with you and the Holy Spirit lives and reigns, one God, for ever and ever. *Amen.*

One or both of the following Lessons, or other appropriate Readings, may follow

Old Testament   Genesis 18:1-8
Epistle   3 John 1-6a, 11, 13-15

Between the Readings, or after the Reading if only one is used, Psalm 112:1-7, or some other psalm or song, may be sung or said.

If there is to be a Communion, a passage from the Gospel is always included. The following are appropriate:

Gospel John 11:5; 12:1-3 *or* Matthew 6:25-33

A homily or brief address may follow.

When appropriate, the Celebrant then says the following invocation

Let the mighty power of the Holy God be present in this place to banish from it every unclean spirit, to cleanse it from every residue of evil, and to make it a secure habitation for *those* who *dwell* in it; in the Name of Jesus Christ our Lord. *Amen.*

If convenient, prayers for the several rooms of the house are offered at this time. The Celebrant, with members of the household (one of them carrying a lighted candle if desired), and others as convenient, move from room to room, concluding the procession in the living room. Meanwhile, those not participating in the procession remain in the living room, praying silently or singing hymns or other suitable songs.

If the procession does not take place here, the service continues with the Blessing of the Home on page 139. The prayers in the separate rooms may be used before or after the service.

The prayers in the rooms may be used in any convenient sequence.

The appointed antiphons may be read or sung by all, or by the celebrant, or by some other person.

At the Entrance

Antiphon

Behold, I stand at the door and knock, says the Lord. If you hear my voice and open the door, I will come into the house, and eat with you, and you with me.

V. The Lord shall watch over your going out and your coming in:
R. From this time forth for evermore.

Let us pray.   *(Silence)*

Sovereign Lord, you are Alpha and Omega, the beginning and the end: Send your *servants* out from this place on many errands, be *their* constant companion in the way, and welcome *them* upon *their* return, so that coming and going *they* may be sustained by your presence, O Christ our Lord. *Amen.*

*

In an Oratory or Chapel, or at a Shrine

Antiphon

Let them make me a sanctuary, that I may dwell in their midst.

V. Lift up your hands in the holy place:
R. And bless the Lord.

Let us pray. *(Silence)*

Almighty God, from you comes every good prayer, and you pour out on those who desire it the spirit of grace and supplication: Deliver your *servants* when *they draw* near to you in this place from coldness of heart and wanderings of mind, that with steadfast thoughts and kindled affections *they* may worship you in spirit and in truth; through Jesus Christ our Lord. *Amen.*

In a Study or Library

Antiphon

Teach us, O Lord, where wisdom is to be found, and show us the place of understanding.

V.   Seek the Lord your God, and you will find him:
R.   Search for him with all your heart and with all your soul.

Let us pray. *(Silence)*

O God of truth, eternal ground of all that is, beyond space and time yet within them, transcending all things yet pervading them: Show yourself to us, for we go about in ignorance; reveal yourself to us, for it is you that we seek, O Triune God, Father, Son, and Holy Spirit. *Amen.*

In a Bedroom

Antiphon

Guide us waking, O Lord, and guard us sleeping, that awake we may watch with Christ, and asleep we may rest in peace.

V.   I lie down and go to sleep:
R.   I wake again, because the Lord sustains me.

Let us pray. *(Silence)*

O God of life and love, the true rest of your people: Sanctify to your *servants their* hours of rest and refreshment, *their* sleeping and *their* waking; and grant that, strengthened by the indwelling of the Holy Spirit, *they* may rise to serve you all the days of *their* life; through Jesus Christ our Lord. *Amen.*

In a Child's Room

Antiphon

Jesus said, Let the children come to me, and do not hinder them; for to those like them belongs the kingdom of heaven.

V.   Praise the Lord, you children of the Lord:
R.   Praise the Name of the Lord.

Let us pray. *(Silence)*

Heavenly Father, your Son our Savior took young children into his arms and blessed them: Embrace the *child* whose room this is with your unfailing love, protect *him* from all danger, and bring *him* in safety to each new day, until *he greets* with joy the great day of your kingdom; through Jesus Christ our Lord. *Amen.*

In a Guest Room

Antiphon

Do not neglect to show hospitality, for thereby some have entertained angels unawares.

V. Open your homes to each other without complaining:
R. Use the gifts you have received from God for the good
   of others.

Let us pray. *(Silence)*

Loving God, you have taught us to welcome one another as
Christ welcomed us: Bless those who from time to time
share the hospitality of this home. May your fatherly care
shield them, the love of your dear Son preserve them from all
evil, and the guidance of your Holy Spirit keep them in the
way that leads to eternal life; through Jesus Christ our Lord.
Amen.

In a Bathroom

Antiphon

I will sprinkle you with clean water, and you will be
cleansed.

V. Let us hold fast the confession of our hope without
   wavering:
R. Having our bodies washed with pure water.

Let us pray. *(Silence)*

O holy God, in the incarnation of your Son our Lord you
made our flesh the instrument of your self-revelation: Give
us a proper respect and reverence for our mortal bodies,
keeping them clean and fair, whole and sound; that,
glorifying you in them, we may confidently await our being
clothed upon with spiritual bodies, when that which is
mortal is transformed by life; through Jesus Christ our Lord.
Amen.

In a Workroom or Workshop

Antiphon

Many there are who rely upon their hands and are skillful in their own work.

V. Prosper, O Lord, the work of our hands:
R. Prosper our handiwork.

Let us pray. *(Silence)*

O God, your blessed Son worked with his hands in the carpenter shop in Nazareth: Be present, we pray, with *those* who *work* in this place, that, laboring as *workers* together with you, *they* may share the joy of your creation; through Jesus Christ our Lord. *Amen.*

In the Kitchen

Antiphon

You shall eat in plenty and be satisfied, and praise the Name of the Lord your God, who has dealt wondrously with you.

V. The eyes of all wait upon you, O Lord:
R. And you give them their food in due season.

Let us pray. *(Silence)*

O Lord our God, you supply every need of ours according to your great riches: Bless the hands that work in this place, and give us grateful hearts for daily bread; through Jesus Christ our Lord. *Amen.*

In a Dining Room or Area

Antiphon

The living God gave you from heaven rain and fruitful seasons, satisfying your hearts with food and gladness.

V. He brings forth food from the earth,
    and wine to gladden our hearts:
R. Oil to make a cheerful countenance,
    and bread to strengthen the heart.

Let us pray. *(Silence)*

Blessed are you, O Lord, King of the universe, for you give us food and drink to sustain our lives: Make us grateful for all your mercies, and mindful of the needs of others; through Jesus Christ our Lord. *Amen.*

In a Terrace or Garden

Antiphon

As the earth puts forth its blossom, or bushes in a garden burst into flower, so shall the Lord God make righteousness and praise blossom before all the nations.

V. My boundaries enclose a pleasant land:
R. Indeed, I have a goodly heritage.

Let us pray. *(Silence)*

Jesus, our good Companion, on many occasions you withdrew with your friends for quiet and refreshment: Be present with your *servants* in this place, to which *they come* for fellowship and recreation; and make of it, we pray, a place of serenity and peace; in your Name we ask it. *Amen.*

In the Living Room or Family Room

Antiphon

Oh, how good and pleasant it is, when God's people live together in unity!

V. Above everything, love one another earnestly:
R. For love covers many sins.

Let us pray. *(Silence)*

Give your blessing, Lord, to all who share this room, that they may be knit together in fellowship here on earth, and joined with the communion of your saints in heaven; through Jesus Christ our Lord. *Amen.*

In those rooms and other places for which no provision has been made in this service, any suitable antiphon, versicle, and prayer may be used.

The Blessing of the Home

When the procession has returned to the living room, or immediately after the homily (and invocation), the Celebrant completes the blessing of the home as follows:

Antiphon

The effect of righteousness will be peace, and the result of righteousness tranquillity and trust for ever. My people will abide in secure dwellings and in quiet resting places.

V. Unless the Lord builds the house:
R. Their labor is in vain who build it.

Let us pray. *(Silence)*

Visit, O blessed Lord, this home with the gladness of your presence. Bless *all* who *live* here with the gift of your love; and grant that *they* may manifest your love [to each other and] to all whose lives *they touch*. May *they* grow in grace and in the knowledge and love of you; guide, comfort, and strengthen *them*; and preserve *them* in peace, O Jesus Christ, now and for ever. *Amen.*

The Celebrant then says to the people

The peace of the Lord be always with you.
And also with you.

The People greet one another in the name of the Lord.

If there is not to be a Communion, the service concludes with the Lord's Prayer and a blessing.

If there is to be a Communion, the Liturgy continues with the Offertory.

Members of the household present the offerings of bread and wine.

The Celebrant continues with one of the authorized Eucharistic Prayers, or with one of the Forms of the Great Thanksgiving from An Order for Celebrating the Holy Eucharist.

If the Great Thanksgiving provides for a Proper Preface, the following may be used

Through Jesus Christ our Lord, who grew to perfect manhood in his parents' home at Nazareth, and in the home of friends in Bethany revealed himself as Life and Resurrection.

In place of the usual postcommunion prayer, the following may be used

How wonderful you are, O gracious God, in all your
dealings with your people! We praise you now, and give you
thanks, because in the blessed Sacrament of the Body and
Blood of our Savior Jesus Christ you have visited this house
and hallowed it by your presence. Stay among us, we pray,
to bind us together in your love and peace. May we serve
you, and others in your name; through Jesus Christ our
Lord. *Amen.*

The service may conclude with a dismissal.

*If there has not been a Communion as part of the service, it is desirable
that there be a celebration of the Holy Eucharist in the home at the
earliest convenient time.*

Blessing of a Pregnant Woman

The following may be used either privately or at a public service.

O Lord and giver of life, receive our prayer for N. and for the child she has conceived, that they may happily come to the time of birth, and serving you in all things may rejoice in your loving providence. We ask this through our Lord Jesus Christ, who lives and reigns with you and the Holy Spirit, one God, now and for ever. *Amen.*

When appropriate, any or all of the following may be added:

Blessed are you, Lord God. You have blessed the union of N. and N. *Amen.*

Blessed are you, Lord God. May your blessing be upon N. and the child she carries. *Amen.*

Blessed are you, Lord God. May this time of pregnancy be for N. and N. months of drawing nearer to you and to one another. *Amen.*

Blessed are you, Lord God. May N. and N.'s experience of birth be full of awe and wonder and the joy of sharing in your creation. *Amen.*

Blessed are you, Lord God. Let the fullness of your blessing be upon those whom we bless in your Name: Father, Son, and Holy Spirit. *Amen.*

The anticipation of birth is an appropriate time for the Minister of the Congregation to discuss with expectant parents the meaning of Baptism.

Anniversary of a Marriage

This form is intended for use in the context of a celebration of the Holy Eucharist. When the form is used at a principal service on a Sunday or Major Holy Day, the Proper of the Day is used. When it is used at other times, the Psalm and Lessons are selected from those recommended for use at the Celebration and Blessing of a Marriage, and one of the following Collects is used for the Collect of the Day.

O gracious and everliving God, look mercifully on N. and N., who come to renew the promises they have made to each other. Grant them your blessing, and assist them with your grace, that with true fidelity and steadfast love they may honor and keep their promises and vows; through Jesus Christ our Savior, who lives and reigns with you, in the unity of the Holy Spirit, one God, for ever and ever. *Amen.*

or this

O God, you have so consecrated the covenant of marriage that in it is represented the spiritual unity between Christ and his Church: Send your blessing upon N. and N., who come to renew their promises to each other, and grant them your grace, that they may so love, honor, and cherish each other in faithfulness and patience, in wisdom and true godliness, that their lives together may be a witness to your love and forgiveness, and that their home may be a haven of blessing and peace; through Jesus Christ our Lord, who lives and reigns with you and the Holy Spirit, one God, now and for ever. *Amen.*

or this

Grant, O God, in your compassion, that N. and N., having taken each other in marriage, and affirming again the covenant which they have made, may grow in forgiveness, loyalty, and love; and come at last to the eternal joys which you have promised through Jesus Christ our Lord; who lives and reigns with you, in the unity of the Holy Spirit, one God, for ever and ever. *Amen.*

Immediately after the Sermon (and the Creed if appointed), the Husband and Wife present themselves before the celebrant, who stands facing the people.

All stand, and the Celebrant addresses the congregation with these or similar words

Friends in Christ, we are gathered together with N. and N., who have come today to give thanks to God for his blessing upon their marriage, and to reaffirm their marriage covenant.

The Celebrant then asks the man

N., do you here, in the presence of God and of this congregation, renew the promises you made when you bound yourself to N. in holy matrimony?

The Man answers

I do.

The Celebrant then asks the woman

N., do you here, in the presence of God and of this congregation, renew the promises you made when you bound yourself to N. in holy matrimony?

The Woman answers

I do.

The Husband and Wife, kneeling or standing, say together

We thank you, most gracious God, for consecrating our
marriage in Christ's Name and presence. Lead us further in
companionship with each other and with you. Give us grace
to live together in love and fidelity, with care for one
another. Strengthen us all our days, and bring us to that holy
table where, with those we love, we will feast for ever in our
heavenly home; through Jesus Christ our Lord. *Amen.*

The Celebrant then blesses them, saying

May God the Father, who at creation ordained that man and
woman become one flesh, keep you one. *Amen.*

May God the Son, who adorned this manner of life by his
first miracle, at the wedding in Cana of Galilee, be present
with you always. *Amen.*

May God the Holy Spirit, who has given you the will to
persevere in your love and in your covenant with each other,
strengthen your bond. *Amen.*

And may God the Holy Trinity, the source of all unity, bless
you this day and for ever. *Amen.*

*The service continues with the Peace, or, at a principal service, with the
Prayers of the People.*

The husband and wife may present the bread and wine at the Offertory.

*If there is not to be a Communion, the service concludes with the Lord's
Prayer and the Peace.*

*When this form is used as an act of reconciliation, the celebrant may
adapt it in consultation with the parties.*

A Public Service of Healing

The service begins as appointed for a celebration of the Holy Eucharist, or with the Penitential Order, or with the following greeting

Celebrant Grace and peace be with you, from God our Father
　　　　　and the Lord Jesus Christ.
People　　And also with you.
Celebrant Let us pray.

The Celebrant says this or some other appropriate Collect

O God of peace, you have taught us that in returning and rest we shall be saved, in quietness and confidence shall be our strength: By the might of your Spirit lift us, we pray, to your presence, where we may be still and know that you are God; through Jesus Christ our Lord, who with you and the Holy Spirit lives and reigns, one God, for ever and ever. *Amen.*

One or two Lessons are read before the Gospel.

Between the Lessons, and before the Gospel, a Psalm, hymn, or anthem may be sung or said.

If the Proper of the Day is not used, the Lessons, Psalm, and Gospel are selected from the Table on page 152.

A sermon or meditation, or a period of silence, or both, may follow the Gospel.

The service continues with the Creed, or with the Prayers of the People.

For the Prayers of the People a Litany of Healing, as follows, may be used.

Litany of Healing

The Celebrant introduces the Litany with this bidding

Let us name before God those for whom we offer our prayers.

The People audibly name those for whom they are interceding.

A Person appointed then leads the Litany

God the Father, your will for all people is health and salvation;
We praise you and thank you, O Lord.

God the Son, you came that we might have life, and might have it more abundantly;
We praise you and thank you, O Lord.

God the Holy Spirit, you make our bodies the temple of your presence;
We praise you and thank you, O Lord.

Holy Trinity, one God, in you we live and move and have our being;
We praise you and thank you , O Lord.

Lord, grant your healing grace to all who are sick, injured, or disabled, that they may be made whole;
Hear us, O Lord of life.

Grant to all who seek your guidance, and to all who are
lonely, anxious, or despondent, a knowledge of your will
and an awareness of your presence;
Hear us, O Lord of life.

Mend broken relationships, and restore those in emotional
distress to soundness of mind and serenity of spirit;
Hear us, O Lord of life.

Bless physicians, nurses, and all others who minister to the
suffering, granting them wisdom and skill, sympathy and
patience;
Hear us, O Lord of life.

Grant to the dying peace and a holy death, and uphold by
the grace and consolation of your Holy Spirit those who are
bereaved;
Hear us, O Lord of life.

Restore to wholeness whatever is broken by human sin, in
our lives, in our nation, and in the world;
Hear us, O Lord of life.

You are the Lord who does wonders:
You have declared your power among the peoples.

With you, O Lord, is the well of life:
And in your light we see light.

Hear us, O Lord of life:
Heal us, and make us whole.

Let us pray.

A period of silence follows.

The Celebrant concludes the Prayers with one of the following or some other suitable Collect:

Almighty God, giver of life and health: Send your blessing on all who are sick, and upon those who minister to them, that all weakness may be vanquished by the triumph of the risen Christ; who lives and reigns for ever and ever. *Amen.*

or this

Heavenly Father, you have promised to hear what we ask in the Name of your Son: Accept and fulfill our petitions, we pray, not as we ask in our ignorance, nor as we deserve in our sinfulness, but as you know and love us in your Son Jesus Christ our Lord. *Amen.*

or this

O Lord our God, accept the fervent prayers of your people; in the multitude of your mercies look with compassion upon us and all who turn to you for help; for you are gracious, O lover of souls, and to you we give glory, Father, Son, and Holy Spirit, now and for ever. *Amen.*

A Confession of Sin follows, if it has not been said at the beginning of the service.

The Celebrant now invites those who wish to receive the laying on of hands (and anointing) to come forward.

If oil for the anointing of the sick is to be blessed, the form on page 455 of the Prayer Book is used.

The following anthem is sung or said

Savior of the world, by your cross and precious blood you have redeemed us;
Save us, and help us, we humbly beseech you, O Lord.

The Celebrant says the following blessing over those who have come forward

The Almighty Lord, who is a strong tower to all who put their trust in him, to whom all things in heaven, on earth, and under the earth bow and obey: Be now and evermore your defense, and make you know and feel that the only Name under heaven given for health and salvation is the Name of our Lord Jesus Christ. *Amen.*

The Celebrant then lays hands on each person (and, having dipped a thumb in the oil of the sick, makes the sign of the cross on their foreheads), and says one of the following:

N., I lay my hands upon you [and anoint you with oil] in the Name of the Father, and of the Son, and of the Holy Spirit, beseeching our Lord Jesus Christ to sustain you with his presence, to drive away all sickness of body and spirit, and to give you that victory of life and peace which will enable you to serve him both now and evermore. *Amen.*

or this

N., I lay my hands upon you [and anoint you with oil] in the Name of our Lord and Savior Jesus Christ, beseeching him to uphold you and fill you with grace, that you may know the healing power of his love. *Amen.*

or this

[N.,] I lay my hands upon you [and anoint you with oil] in the Name of the Father, and of the Son, and of the Holy Spirit. *Amen.*

or prayer may be offered for each person individually according to that person's need, with laying on of hands (and anointing).

Lay persons with a gift of healing may join the celebrant in the laying on of hands.

The service continues with the exchange of the Peace.

If there is not to be a Communion, the service concludes with the Lord's Prayer and the prayer and blessing given below.

If the Eucharist is to be celebrated, the Liturgy continues with the Offertory.

In place of the usual postcommunion prayer (or, if there has not been a Communion, after the Lord's Prayer), the following prayer is said

Almighty and eternal God, so draw our hearts to you, so guide our minds, so fill our imaginations, so control our wills, that we may be wholly yours, utterly dedicated to you; and then use us, we pray, as you will, and always to your glory and the welfare of your people; through our Lord and Savior Jesus Christ. *Amen.*

The Celebrant pronounces this blessing

May God the Father bless you, God the Son heal you, God the Holy Spirit give you strength. May God the holy and undivided Trinity guard your body, save your soul, and bring you safely to his heavenly country; where he lives and reigns for ever and ever. *Amen.*

A Deacon, or the Celebrant, dismisses the people.

A Table of Suggested Lessons and Psalms

Old Testament

Exodus 16:13-15(Manna in the wilderness)
1 Kings 17:17-24 (Elijah restores the widow's son to life)
2 Kings 5:9-14 (Healing of Naaman)
2 Kings 20:1-5 (I have heard your prayer . . . I will heal you)
Isaiah 11:1-3a (The gifts of the Spirit)

Isaiah 42:1-7 (The suffering servant)
Isaiah 53:3-5 (With his stripes are we healed)
Isaiah 61:1-3 (Good tidings to the afflicted)

Psalms

Psalm 13 (My heart is joyful because of your saving help)
Psalm 20:1-6 (May the Lord answer you in the day of trouble)
Psalm 23 (You have anointed my head with oil)
Psalm 27   *or*   27:1-7, 9, 18 (The Lord is the strength of my life)
Psalm 91 (He will give his angels charge over you)
Psalm 103 (He forgives all your sins)
Psalm 121 (My help comes from the Lord)
Psalm 130 (My soul waits for the Lord)
Psalm 139:1-17 (Where can I go from your Spirit?)
Psalm 145:14-22 (The eyes of all wait on you, O Lord)
Psalm 146 (Happy are they who have the God of Jacob for their help)

New Testament

Acts 3:1-10 (Peter and John heal the lame man)
Acts 5:12-16 (Healings in Jerusalem; Peter's shadow)
Acts 10:36-43 (Apostolic preaching: He went about . . . healing)
Acts 16:16-18 (The slave girl with the spirit of divination)
Romans 8:18-23 (We await the redemption of our bodies)
Romans 8:31-39 (Nothing can separate us from the love of God)
2 Corinthians 1:3-5 (God comforts us in affliction)
Colossians 1:11-20 (May you be strengthened with all power)
Hebrews 12:1-2 (Looking to Jesus, the perfecter of our faith)
James 5:(13) 14-16 (Is any among you sick?)
1 John 5:13-15 (That you may know that you have eternal life)

The Gospel

Matthew 9:2-8 (Your sins are forgiven)
Matthew 26:26-30, 36-39 (The Last Supper: Not as I will)
Mark 1:21-28 (Jesus heals the man with the unclean spirit)
Mark 1:29-34a (Jesus heals Peter's mother-in-law and others)
Mark 5:1-20 (Healing of Gerasene demoniac)

Mark 5:22-24 (Healing of Jairus' daughter)
Mark 6:7, 12-13 (They anointed with oil many that were sick)
Luke 17:11-19 (Your faith has made you well)
John 5:1b-9 (Do you want to be healed?)
John 6:47-51 (I am the bread of life)
John 9:1-11 (Healing of the man born blind)

Concerning Exorcism

The practice of expelling evil spirits by means of prayer and set formulas derives its authority from the Lord himself who identified these acts as signs of his messiahship. Very early in the life of the Church the development and exercise of such rites were reserved to the bishop, at whose discretion they might be delegated to selected presbyters and others deemed competent.

In accordance with this established tradition, those who find themselves in need of such a ministry should make the fact known to the bishop, through their parish priest, in order that the bishop may determine whether exorcism is needed, who is to perform the rite, and what prayers or other formularies are to be used.

Burial of One Who Does Not Profess the Christian Faith

This anthem; and any of the following Psalms, Lessons, and Prayers; and the form of Committal given below may be used with the Order for Burial on page 506 of the Prayer Book.

Opening Anthem

The steadfast love of the Lord never ceases,
his mercies never come to an end;
they are new every morning;
great is his faithfulness.
The Lord will not cast off for ever.
Though he cause grief, he will have compassion
according to the abundance of his steadfast love;
The Lord does not willingly afflict or grieve his children.

Lessons and Psalms

Ecclesiastes 3:1-11 (For everything there is a season)
Ecclesiastes 12:1-7 (Remember your Creator in the days of your youth)
Psalm 23 (The Lord is my shepherd)
Psalm 90 (Lord, you have been our refuge)
Psalm 121 (I lift up my eyes to the hills)
Psalm 130 (Out of the depths have I called to you, O Lord)
Romans 8:35-39 (Who shall separate us from the love of Christ?)
John 10:11-16 (I am the good shepherd)

Prayers

For the Deceased

Almighty God, we entrust all who are dear to us to your
never-failing care and love, for this life and the life to come,
knowing that you are doing for them better things than we
can desire or pray for; through Jesus Christ our Lord. *Amen.*

Into your hands, O God, we commend our *brother, N.,* as
into the hands of a faithful Creator and most loving Savior.
In your infinite goodness, wisdom, and power, work in *him*
the merciful purpose of your perfect will, through Jesus
Christ our Lord. *Amen.*

For those who mourn

O God of grace and glory, we remember before you this day
our brother (sister), *N.* We thank you for giving *him* to us,
his family and friends, to know and to love as a companion
on our earthly pilgrimage. In your boundless compassion,
console us who mourn. Give us quiet confidence that we
may continue our course in faith; through Jesus Christ our
Lord. *Amen.*

O merciful Father, you have taught us in your holy Word
that you do not willingly afflict or grieve your children:
Look with pity upon the sorrows of your servants for whom
our prayers are offered. Remember them, O Lord, in mercy,
nourish their souls with patience, comfort them with a sense
of your goodness, lift up your countenance upon them, and
give them peace; through Jesus Christ our Lord. *Amen.*

Almighty God, Father of mercies and giver of comfort: Deal graciously, we pray, with all who mourn; that, casting all their care on you, they may know the consolation of your love; through Jesus Christ our Lord. *Amen.*

Most merciful God, whose wisdom is beyond our understanding, deal graciously with *N.N.* in *their* grief. Surround *them* with your love, that *they* may not be overwhelmed by *their* loss, but have confidence in your goodness, and strength to meet the days to come; through Jesus Christ our Lord. *Amen.*

For the Christian community

Most loving Father, whose will it is for us to give thanks for all things, to fear nothing but the loss of you, and to cast all our care on you who care for us: Preserve us from faithless fears and worldly anxieties, that no clouds of this mortal life may hide from us the light of that love which is immortal, and which you have manifested to us in your Son Jesus Christ our Lord. *Amen.*

Almighty God, give us grace to cast away the works of darkness, and put on the armor of light, now in the time of this mortal life in which your Son Jesus Christ came to visit us in great humility; that in the last day, when he shall come again in his glorious majesty to judge both the living and the dead, we may rise to the life immortal; through him who lives and reigns for ever and ever. *Amen.*

The Committal

Holy God, Holy and Mighty, Holy Immortal One, have mercy upon us.

You only are immortal, the creator and maker of mankind; and we are mortal, formed of the earth, and to earth shall we return. For so did you ordain when you created me, saying, "You are dust, and to dust you shall return." All of us go down to the dust; yet even at the grave we make our song: Alleluia, alleluia, alleluia.

Holy God, Holy and Mighty, Holy Immortal One, have mercy upon us.

Commissioning for Lay Ministries in the Church

The Ministers of the Church are lay persons, bishops, priests, and deacons. Lay persons are commissioned for their ministry by the Sacrament of Holy Baptism, and no form of commissioning for special functions is necessary. The form which follows is intended for use when a public recognition of a special function is desired. It may be adapted for the admission of persons to ministries not provided for in the text.

*This form may be used following the homily (and Creed) at the
Eucharist, or at the time of the hymn or anthem following the Collects in
Morning or Evening Prayer, or separately.*

*After the Examination, each group of candidates is presented separately
by an appointed sponsor.*

*Symbols appropriate to the ministry may be given to the candidates as
they are commissioned.*

*When the number of candidates for any office is large, it is sufficient to
say the sentence of commissioning once over the entire group, but it is
desirable that each person be greeted individually (and be given an
appropriate symbol).*

The Examination

*The congregation being seated, the celebrant stands in full view of the
people. The sponsors and candidates stand facing the celebrant.*

The Celebrant says these or similar words

Brothers and Sisters in Christ Jesus, we are all baptized by
the one Spirit into one Body, and given gifts for a variety of
ministries for the common good. Our purpose is to
commission *these persons* in the Name of God and of this
congregation to a special ministry to which *they are* called.

The Celebrant asks the sponsor or sponsors

Are these persons you are to present prepared by a commitment to Christ as Lord, by regular attendance at worship, and by the knowledge of *their* duties, to exercise *their* ministry to the honor of God, and the well-being of his Church?

Sponsor I believe *they are*.

The Celebrant then says these or similar words

You have been called to a ministry in this congregation. Will you, as long as you are engaged in this work, perform it with diligence?

Candidate I will.

Celebrant Will you faithfully and reverently execute the duties of your ministry to the honor of God, and the benefit of the members of this congregation?
Candidate I will.

When used as a separate service, a Scripture reading from the list on page 176 (and a homily) follows here.

The Commissioning

One or more of the following forms is used as appropriate.

The appointed antiphons may be read or sung by all, or by the celebrant, or by some other person.

1. Wardens and Members of the Vestry

Sponsor   I present to you *these persons* to be admitted to the ministry of Warden (Member of the Vestry) in this congregation.

Antiphon

The Lord gives wisdom; from his mouth come knowledge and understanding; he stores up sound wisdom for the upright; he is a shield to those who walk in integrity.

V.   I am your servant; grant me understanding:
R.   That I may know your decrees.

Let us pray.   *(Silence)*

O Eternal God, the foundation of all wisdom and the source of all courage: Enlighten with your grace the Wardens and Vestry of this congregation, and so rule their minds, and guide their counsels, that in all things they may seek your glory and promote the mission of your Church; through Jesus Christ our Lord. *Amen.*

In the Name of God and of this congregation. I commission you [N.] as Warden (Member of the Vestry) in this *Parish* [and give you this _____ as a token of your ministry].

2. Deputies to the General Convention, or Delegates to Diocesan Convention

Sponsor   I present to you *these persons,* duly elected by the people and clergy of this diocese as *Deputies* to the General Convention, to be commissioned for *their* ministry.

or the following

Sponsor   I present to you *these persons*, duly elected as
Delegates to Diocesan Convention, to be
commissioned for *their* ministry.

Antiphon

Call a solemn assembly, gather the people, assemble the
elders, and sanctify the congregation.

V.   Save your people, Lord, and bless your inheritance.
R.   Govern and uphold them, now and always.

Let us pray.   *(Silence)*

Eternal Lord God, who by the Holy Spirit presided at the
council of the Apostles to guide them in all knowledge and
truth: Be present with the *Deputies of this diocese soon to be
assembled in General Convention.* In the passions of debate
give them a quiet spirit, in the complexities of the issues give
them clear minds, and in the moments of decision give them
courageous hearts. Guide them in all things to seek only
your glory and the good of your Church; through Jesus
Christ our Lord. *Amen.*

In the Name of God and of this diocese (congregation), I
commission you [*N.*] as *Deputies* to General Convention
(*Delegates* to Diocesan Convention) [and give you this
_____ as a token of your ministry].

3. Servers at the Altar

Sponsor   I present to you *these persons* to be admitted to the
ministry of Server in this congregation.

Antiphon

Do not be negligent, for the Lord has chosen you to stand in his presence, to minister to him, and to be his minister.

V. I will go to the altar of God:
R. To the God of my joy and gladness.

Let us pray. *(Silence)*

O God, our gracious Father: Bless the servers of your Church that they may so serve before your earthly altar in reverence and holiness, that they may attain, with all your saints and angels, the joy of serving you and worshiping you before your Heavenly Altar; through Jesus Christ our Lord. *Amen.*

In the Name of God and of this congregation, I commission you [N.] as Server in this *Parish*, [and give you this ⎯⎯⎯⎯ as a token of your ministry].

4. Altar Guild Members and Sacristans

Sponsor I present to you *these persons* to be admitted to the ministry of the Altar Guild (Sacristan) in this congregation.

Antiphon

The Levites were responsible for the ark, the table, the lampstand, the altars, and the vessels of the sanctuary with which the priests minister.

V. In the temple of the Lord all are crying, "Glory!"
R. Holiness adorns your house, O Lord, for ever.

Let us pray. *(Silence)*

O God, you accepted the service of Levites in your temple, and your Son was pleased to accept the loving service of his friends: Bless the ministry of *these persons* and give *them* grace, that *they*, caring for the vessels and vestments of your worship and the adornment of your sanctuary, may make the place of your presence glorious; through Jesus Christ our Lord. *Amen.*

In the Name of God and of this congregation, I commission you [N.] as member of the Altar Guild (Sacristan) of this *Parish* [and give you this _____ as a token of your ministry].

5. Catechists or Teachers

Sponsor   I present to you *these persons* to be admitted to the ministry of Catechist (Teacher) in this congregation.

Antiphon

The words which I command you this day shall be upon your hearts; and you shall teach them diligently to your children, and shall talk of them when you sit in your house, and when you walk by the way, and when you lie down, and when you rise.

V.   We will recount to generations to come the praiseworthy deeds and the power of the Lord:
R.   And the wonderful works he has done.

Let us pray. *(Silence)*

God of all wisdom and knowledge, give your blessing and guidance to all who teach in your Church, that by word and example they may lead those whom they teach to the knowledge and love of you; through Jesus Christ our Lord. *Amen*.

In the Name of God and of this congregation, I commission you [N.] as Catechist (Teacher) in this *Parish* [and give you this _____ as a token of your ministry].

6. Evangelists

Sponsor   I present to you *these persons* to be admitted to the ministry of Evangelist in this congregation.

Antiphon

The gifts of the Lord were that some should be apostles, some prophets, some evangelists, some pastors and teachers, to equip the saints for the work of ministry, for building up the body of Christ.

V.   Declare his glory among the nations and his wonders among the people:
R.   Tell it out among the nations: "The Lord is King!"

Let us pray.   *(Silence)*

Gracious Father, your Son before he ascended to glory declared that your people would receive power from the Holy Spirit to bear witness to him to the ends of the earth: Be present with all who go forth in his Name. Let your love shine through their witness, so that the blind may see, the deaf hear, the lame walk, the dead be raised up, and the poor have the good news preached to them; through Jesus Christ our Lord. *Amen*.

In the Name of God and of this congregation, I commission you [N.,] as Evangelist in this *Parish* [and give you this _____ as a token of your ministry].

7. Singers

Sponsor   I present to you *these persons* to be admitted to the ministry of Singer (Cantor) (Chorister) in this congregation.

Antiphon

Sing to the Lord and bless his Name; proclaim the good news of his salvation from day to day.

V.   Come let us sing to the Lord:
R.   Let us shout for joy to the Rock of our salvation.

Let us pray.   *(Silence)*

O God, who inspired David the King both to write songs and to appoint singers for your worship: Give grace to the *singers* in your Church, that with psalms, and hymns, and spiritual songs, they may sing and make music to the glory of your Name; through Jesus Christ our Lord. *Amen.*

In the Name of God and of this congregation, I commission you [N.] as a *Singer* in this *Parish* [and give this _____ as a token of your ministry].

8. Directors of Music, Organists, and other Musicians

Sponsor   I present to you *this person* to be admitted to the
ministry of *Organist and Choirmaster* in this
congregation.

Antiphon

David commanded the chief of the Levites to appoint
musicians who should play loudly on musical instruments,
on harps and lyres and cymbals, to raise sounds of joy.

V.   When the song was raised in the praise of the Lord:
R.   The glory of the Lord filled the house of God.

Let us pray.   *(Silence)*

O God, whom saints and angels delight to worship in
heaven, be ever present with your servants who seek through
music to perfect the praises offered by your people on earth;
and grant them even now glimpses of your beauty, and make
them worthy at length to behold it unveiled for evermore;
through Jesus Christ our Lord. *Amen.*

In the Name of God and of this congregation, I commission
you [N.] as *Organist and Choirmaster* in this *Parish* [and
give you this _____ as a token of your ministry].

9. Lectors

Sponsor   I present to you *these persons* to be admitted to the
ministry of Lector in this congregation.

Antiphon

They read from the book, from the law of God, clearly; and they gave all the sense, so that the people understood the reading.

V. Your word is a lantern to my feet:
R. And a light upon my path.

Let us pray. *(Silence)*

Almighty God, whose blessed Son read the Holy Scriptures in the synagogue: Look graciously upon the lectors of your Church, and so enlighten them with wisdom and understanding that they may read your holy Word to the glory of your Name, and for the building up of your people; through Jesus Christ our Lord. *Amen.*

In the Name of God and of this congregation, I commission you [N.] as Lector in this *Parish* [and I give you this _____ as a token of your ministry].

10. Those Who Administer the Chalice

Sponsor   I present to you *these persons* who *have* been chosen and licensed to administer the chalice in this congregation.

Antiphon

The cup of blessing which we bless is a sharing in the Blood of Christ. The bread which we break is a sharing in the Body of Christ.

V. As often as you eat this bread and drink this cup:
R. You proclaim the Lord's death until he comes.

Let us pray. *(Silence)*

Grant, Almighty God, that those who minister the cup of blessing may live in love and holiness according to your commandment, and at the last come to the joy of your heavenly feast with all your saints in light; through Jesus Christ our Lord. *Amen.*

In the Name of God and of this congregation, I commission you [N.] to administer the chalice in this *Parish* [and give you this _____ as a token of your ministry].

11. Licensed Lay Readers

Sponsor   I present to you *this person* licensed by the Bishop for the ministry of Lay Reader in this diocese.

Antiphon

There are varieties of gifts, but the same Spirit; and there are varieties of service, but the same Lord; and there are varieties of working, but it is the same God who inspires them all in everyone.

V.   Let the word of Christ dwell in you richly:
R.   Do everything in the name of the Lord Jesus.

Let us pray *(Silence)*

Look with favor upon those whom you have called, O Lord, to be Lay Readers in your Church; and grant that they may be so filled with your Holy Spirit that, seeking your glory and the salvation of souls, they may minister your Word with steadfast devotion, and by the constancy of their faith and the innocency of their lives may adorn in all things the doctrine of Christ our Savior; who lives and reigns for ever and ever. *Amen.*

In the Name of God and of this congregation, I commission
you [N.] as Licensed Lay Reader [and give you this
_____ as a token of your ministry].

12. Parish Visitors

Sponsor   I present to you *these persons* to be admitted to the
ministry of Parish Visitor in this congregation.

Antiphon

Religion that is pure and undefiled before God and the
Father is this: to visit orphans and widows in their affliction
and to keep oneself unstained from the world.

V.   Let not the needy, O Lord, be forgotten:
R.   Nor the hope of the poor be taken away.

Let us pray.   *(Silence)*

O God, your Son Jesus Christ said that we minister to him
when we clothe the naked, give food to the hungry and
drink to the thirsty, and visit the sick and imprisoned: Go
with all those who, following the command of your Christ,
visit your people in his Name; who lives and reigns for ever
and ever. *Amen.*

In the Name of God and of this congregation, I commission
you [N.] as Visitor in this *Parish* [and give you this
_____ as a token of your ministry].

13. Members of Prayer Groups

Sponsor   I present to you *these persons* who *have* accepted a
special ministry of intercessory prayer in this
congregation.

Antiphon

Rejoice always, pray constantly, give thanks in all circumstances; for this is the will of God in Christ Jesus for you.

V.   In truth God has heard me:
R.   He has attended to the voice of my prayer.

Let us pray.   *(Silence)*

O God, whose Son our Lord on the night of his betrayal prayed for all his disciples: Hear the prayers of all those who accept the work and ministry of intercession on behalf of others, that the needs of many may be met and your will be done; through Jesus Christ our great High Priest. *Amen.*

[*N.,*] In the Name of God and of this congregation, I recognize your ministry of intercession in this *Parish* [and give you this _____ as a token of your ministry].

14. Parish Canvassers

Sponsor   I present to you *these persons* who *have* accepted the ministry of Canvasser in this congregation.

Antiphon

God, who supplies seed for sowing and bread for eating, will supply the seed you need, and produce a rich harvest.

V.   Each one must do as he has made up his mind, not reluctantly or under compulsion:
R.   For God loves a cheerful giver.

Let us pray.   *(Silence)*

Lord Jesus Christ, you sent laborers to prepare for your coming: Be with all those who go forth in your Name, that by their witness and commitment the hearts of many will be turned to you; who live and reign for ever and ever. *Amen.*

In the Name of God and of this congregation, I commission you [N.] as Canvasser in this *Parish* [and give you this _____ as a token of your ministry].

15. Officers of Church Organizations

Sponsor   I present to you *these persons* to be installed as _____ of _____ in this congregation.

Antiphon

God will not overlook your work and the love which you show for his sake.

V.   Teach me to do what pleases you, for you are my God:
R.   Let your good Spirit lead me on level ground.

Let us pray.   *(Silence)*

Regard, O Lord, our supplications, and confirm with your heavenly benediction your *servants* whom we admit today to the ministry (office) of _____; that with sincere devotion of mind and body *they* may offer you a service acceptable to your divine Majesty; through Jesus Christ our Lord. *Amen.*

In the Name of God and of this congregation, I admit you [N.] to the office of _____ of _____ [and give you this _____ as a token of your office].

16. Other Lay Ministries

Sponsor   I present to you *these persons* to be admitted to the ministry of _____ in this congregation.

The following, or some other antiphon, versicle and Collect may be used.

Antiphon

You are my witnesses, says the Lord, and my servants whom I have chosen.

V.   Give thanks to the Lord and call upon his Name:
R.   Make known his deeds among the peoples.

Let us pray.   *(Silence)*

Have regard to our supplication, O gracious Lord, and confirm with your heavenly benediction your *servants* commissioned to minister in your Church, that with sincere devotion of mind and body *they* may offer acceptable service to you; through Jesus Christ our Lord. *Amen.*

In the Name of God and of this congregation, I commission you [N.] as _____ in this *Parish* [and give you this _____ as a token of your ministry].

When used with the Eucharist, the service continues with (the Prayers of the People and) the exchange of the Peace.

The following Collect may be used at the conclusion of the Prayers of the People

O Lord, without whom our labor is lost: We beseech you to prosper all works in your Church undertaken according to your holy will. Grant to your workers a pure intention, a patient faith, sufficient success on earth, and the blessedness of serving you in heaven; through Jesus Christ our Lord. *Amen.*

When used with the Daily Office, the service continues with the preceding prayer and the exchange of the Peace.

When used separately, it ends with the preceding prayer, the Lord's Prayer, the exchange of the Peace, and a blessing.

Scripture Readings

When used as a separate service, one of the following readings may be used at the discretion of the celebrant:

Numbers 11:16-17 (Gather for me seventy men of the elders of Israel.)
Deuteronomy 4:1-2, 9 (Give heed to the statutes and ordinances which I teach you.)
1 Chronicles 9:26-30, 32 (Some of them had charge of the utensils of service.)
Nehemiah 8:1-4a, 5-6, 8 (Ezra reads the Law of Moses to the people.)
Romans 12:6-12 (Having gifts that differ according to the grace given.)
2 Corinthians 4:2, 5-6 (Having this ministry by the mercy of God.)
Colossians 3:12-17 (Sing psalms and hymns and spiritual songs.)
Hebrew 6:9-12 (God is not so unjust as to overlook your work and love.)
Matthew 5:14-16 (You are the light of the world.)
Mark 4:2-9 (A sower went forth to sow.)
Luke 12:35-37 (He will come and serve them.)
John 6: (1-7) 8-13 (There is a lad here who has five barley loaves.)

Dedication of Church Furnishings and Ornaments

In accordance with a venerable tradition, church furnishings and ornaments are consecrated by being put to the use for which they were intended. If a rite of dedication is desired, one of the following forms may be used after the sermon (and Creed) at the Eucharist, or at the Daily Office at the time of the hymn or anthem following the Collects.

It is appropriate, when the object to be dedicated is fixed, that there be a procession to that place. If the procession is to a distant place, an anthem (the text of which may be the appointed antiphon), psalm, or hymn may be sung. When the object is portable, it should be brought to the Altar and presented to the celebrant.

The appointed antiphons may be read or sung by all, or by the celebrant, or by some other person.

If a longer form is desired, the presentation, versicles, and prayers on pages 193-194 may be used in connection with the proper form.

1. An Altar   (*Reserved to the Bishop*)

The dedication of an Altar takes place immediately before the Peace.

Antiphon

Arise, go to Bethel, and dwell there, and make there an altar to our God.

V.   I will go to the altar of God:
R.   To the God of my joy and gladness.

Let us pray.   (*Silence*)

The Bishop, standing at the Table with arms extended, says

We praise you, Almighty and eternal God, that for us and our salvation, you sent your Son Jesus Christ to be born among us, that through him we might become your sons and daughters.
Blessed be your Name, Lord God.

We praise you for his life on earth, and for his death upon the cross, through which he offered himself as a perfect sacrifice.
Blessed be your Name, Lord God.

We praise you for raising him from the dead, and for exalting him to be our great High Priest.
Blessed be your Name, Lord God.

We praise you for sending your Holy Spirit to make us holy, and to unite us in your holy Church.
Blessed be your Name, Lord God.

The Bishop lays a hand upon the Table, and continues

Lord God, hear us. Sanctify this Table dedicated to you. Let it be to us a sign of the heavenly Altar where your saints and angels praise you for ever. Accept here the continual recalling of the sacrifice of your Son. Grant that all who eat and drink at this holy Table may be fed and refreshed by his flesh and blood, be forgiven for their sins, united with one another, and strengthened for your service.
Blessed be your Name, Father, Son, and Holy Spirit; now and for endless ages. Amen.

Bells may then be rung and music played. If desired, the Bishop may cense the Altar. Members of the congregation then vest it, place the vessels on it, and light the candles. The Liturgy then continues with the Peace.

2. A Font   (*Reserved to the Bishop*)

It is desirable that the consecration of a Font take place at a service of public Baptism, in which case the following is inserted immediately before the Thanksgiving over the Water on page 306. Otherwise, it takes place as described on pages 177-178 of this book.

Antiphon

Repent and be baptized every one of you in the Name of Jesus Christ.

V. All of us who are baptized into Christ:
R. Have clothed ourselves with Christ.

Let us pray. *(Silence)*

Father, we thank you that through the waters of Baptism we die to sin and are made new in Christ. Grant through your Spirit that those baptized here may enjoy the liberty and splendor of the children of God; through Jesus Christ our Lord. *Amen.*

We dedicate this Font in the Name of the Father, and of the Son, and of the Holy Spirit. *Amen.*

If desired, the Bishop may cense the Font.

When there are persons to be baptized, water is now poured into the Font, and the Bishop proceeds to the Thanksgiving over the Water.

If the consecration of the Font takes place apart from the service of Holy Baptism, (water may be poured into the Font and) the Bishop says

	The Lord be with you.
People	And also with you.
Bishop	Let us give thanks to the Lord our God.
People	It is right to give him thanks and praise.

We thank you, Almighty God, for the gift of water. Over it the Holy Spirit moved in the beginning of creation. Through it you led the children of Israel out of their bondage in Egypt into the land of promise. In it your Son Jesus received the baptism of John and was anointed by the Holy Spirit as the Messiah, the Christ, to lead us, through his death and resurrection, from the bondage of sin into everlasting life.

We thank you, Father, for the water of Baptism. In it we are buried with Christ in his death. By it we share in his resurrection. Through it we are reborn by the Holy Spirit. Therefore in joyful obedience to your Son, we bring into his fellowship those who come to him in faith, baptizing them in the Name of the Father, and of the Son, and of the Holy Spirit.

Grant, by the power of your Holy Spirit, that those who here are cleansed from sin and born again may continue for ever in the risen life of Jesus Christ our Savior.

To him, to you, and to the Holy Spirit, be all honor and glory, now and for ever. *Amen.*

3. Chalices and Patens   (*Traditionally reserved to the Bishop*)

Antiphon

Taste and see that the Lord is good; happy are they who trust in him.

V.   The cup of blessing which we bless is a sharing in the Blood of Christ.
R.   The bread which we break is a sharing in the Body of Christ.

Let us pray. *(Silence)*

Almighty God, whose blessed Son instituted the Sacrament of his Body and Blood: Grant that all who receive the holy Mysteries from *these vessels*, which we now consecrate for use in your Church, may be sustained by his presence and enjoy for ever his heavenly benediction; who lives and reigns in glory everlasting. *Amen.*

4. A Bell   (*Traditionally reserved to the Bishop*)

Antiphon

Their sound has gone out into all lands, and their message to the ends of the world.

V.   I call to you, my people:
R.   My voice is to the children of God.

Let us pray. *(Silence)*

O God, accept our offering of this bell, which we consecrate today [and to which we give the name _____]: Grant that in this generation and in those that are to come, its voice may continually call your people to praise and worship; through Jesus Christ our Lord. *Amen.*

5. A Cross

Antiphon

We will glory in the cross of our Lord Jesus Christ, in whom is our salvation, our life and resurrection.

V.   Christ for us became obedient unto death:
R.   Even death on a cross.

Let us pray.   *(Silence)*

O gracious God, who in your mercy ordained that your Son should suffer death on a cross of shame: We thank you that it has become for us the sign of his triumph and the banner of our salvation; and we pray that this cross may draw our hearts to him, who leads us to the glory of your kingdom; where you live and reign for ever and ever. *Amen.*

6. Candlesticks and Lamps

Antiphon

Before the throne burn seven lamps of fire, which are the seven spirits of God.

V.   You, O Lord, are my lamp:
R.   My God, you make my darkness bright.

Let us pray.   *(Silence)*

O heavenly Father, who revealed to us the vision of your Son in the midst of the candlesticks, and of your Spirit in seven lamps of fire before your throne: Grant that *these lights (lamps),* to be kindled for your glory, may be to us a sign of your presence and the promise of eternal light; through Jesus Christ our Lord. *Amen.*

7. Altar Cloths and Hangings

Antiphon

This is the offering which you shall receive from the people: gold, silver, and bronze, blue and purple and scarlet cloth, and finely woven linen.

V.   O Lord my God, how excellent is your greatness:
R.   You are clothed with majesty and splendor.

Let us pray.   *(Silence)*

O glorious God, all your works proclaim your perfect
beauty: Accept our offering of this _____, and grant
that it may adorn this sanctuary and show forth your glory;
through Jesus Christ our Lord. *Amen.*

8. A Service Book

Antiphon

Glorify the Lord, all you works of the Lord; praise him and
highly exalt him for ever.

V.   All kings shall bow down before him:
R.   All nations shall do him service.

Let us pray.   *(Silence)*

Bless us, O Lord of hosts, as we use this _____ which
we dedicate to your service, and grant that as your saints
and angels always serve you in heaven, so we may worship
you acceptably on earth; through Jesus Christ our Lord.
Amen.

9. A Bible, Lectionary, or Gospel Book

Antiphon

Whatever was written in former days was written for our
instruction, that by steadfastness and by the encouragement
of the Scriptures we might have hope.

V. Jesus opened their minds:
R. To understand the Scriptures.

Let us pray. (*Silence*)

O heavenly Father, whose blessed Son taught the disciples in
all the Scriptures the things concerning himself: Accept this
_____ which we dedicate here today, and grant that we
may so diligently search your holy Word that we may find in
it the wisdom that leads to salvation; through Jesus Christ
our Lord. *Amen.*

10. A Repository for the Scriptures

Antiphon

When Moses finished writing down these laws in a book, he
gave command to the Levites: Take this book and put it
beside the ark of the covenant of the Lord your God.

V. Our hearts burned within us:
R. When Jesus opened to us the Scriptures.

Let us pray. (*Silence*)

Almighty God, who declared your will to the prophets and
sages of Israel, and revealed your glory in the Word made
flesh: Accept, we pray, this repository for the Holy
Scriptures, and grant that through prayer and worship we
may know you as you speak to us today; through Jesus
Christ our Lord. *Amen.*

11. An Aumbry or Tabernacle for the Sacrament

Antiphon

Aaron shall set the bread before the Lord on a table of pure gold, on behalf of the people of Israel, as a covenant for ever.

V. As often as you eat this bread and drink this cup:
R. You proclaim the Lord's death until he comes.

Let us pray. *(Silence)*

O Lord God, Father of our Savior Jesus Christ, who before his passion instituted the Sacrament of his Body and Blood: Grant that in this aumbry (tabernacle) which we set apart today, the outward signs of his covenant may be kept in safety, and that we may show forth his death and resurrection until he comes in glory; who lives and reigns for ever and ever. *Amen.*

12. An Aumbry for the Oils

Antiphon

The Israelites and Levites shall bring grain, new wine, and oil to the rooms where the vessels of the sanctuary are kept.

V. You have anointed my head with oil:
R. My cup is running over.

Let us pray. *(Silence)*

O Lord God of hosts, who commanded priests of the Old Covenant to set apart oil for the anointing of kings and priests, and by your Apostle James commanded the presbyters of your Church to anoint the sick: We here offer to you this aumbry for the safe-keeping of the oils set apart for the anointing of baptism and for the ministry of healing; through him who was anointed as the Christ, and who lives and reigns for ever and ever. *Amen.*

13. An Ambo (Lectern-Pulpit)

Antiphon

Jesus, as his custom was, went into the synagogue on the Sabbath day and stood up to read.

V. Your word is a lantern to our feet:
R. And a light upon our path.

Let us pray. *(Silence)*

Almighty God, in every age you have spoken through the voices of prophets, pastors, and teachers: Purify the lives and lips of those who read and proclaim your holy Word from this *ambo* which we dedicate today, that your word only may be proclaimed, and your word only may be heard; through Jesus Christ our Lord. *Amen.*

14. Chairs, Benches, and Prayer Desks

Antiphon

Round the heavenly throne were twenty-four other thrones, on which were seated twenty-four elders.

V. The Lord has set his throne in heaven:
R. And his kingship has dominion over all.

Let us pray. *(Silence)*

O Lord God Almighty, you disclosed in a vision the elders seated around your throne: Accept *this chair* for the use of those called to minister in your earthly sanctuary, and grant that those who serve you here may do so with reverence and love, to your honor and glory; through Jesus Christ our Lord. *Amen.*

15. A Stained Glass Window

Antiphon

I will make your windows of agates, and all your borders of pleasant stones.

V. Look upon the rainbow, and praise him who made it:
R. How beautiful it is in its brightness.

Let us pray. *(Silence)*

O Lord God, the whole world is filled with the radiance of your glory: Accept our offering of this window which we now dedicate to you for the adornment of this place and the inspiration of your people. Grant that as the light shines through it in many colors, so our lives may show forth the beauty of your manifold gifts of grace; through Jesus Christ our Lord. *Amen.*

16. Pictures and Statues

Antiphon

Christ is the icon of the invisible God; all things were created through him and for him.

V.   The Word became flesh:
R.   And dwelt among us.

Let us pray.   *(Silence)*

Almighty God, whose Son our Savior manifested your glory in his flesh, and sanctified the outward and visible to be a means to perceive realities unseen: Accept, we pray, this representation of _____ ; and grant that as we look upon it, our hearts may be drawn to things which can be seen only by the eye of faith; through Jesus Christ our Lord. *Amen.*

17. An Organ or Other Musical Instrument

Antiphon

They sing to the tambourine and the lyre, and rejoice to the sound of the pipes.

V.   Praise him with the sound of the trumpet:
R.   Praise him with lyre and harp.

Let us pray.   *(Silence)*

O Lord, before whose throne trumpets sound, and saints and angels sing the songs of Moses and the Lamb: Accept this *organ* for the worship of your temple, that with the voice of music we may proclaim your praise and tell it abroad; through Jesus Christ our Lord. *Amen.*

18. A Vessel for Incense

Antiphon

Another angel came and stood at the altar with a golden censer; he was given much incense, and the smoke of the incense rose with the prayers of the saints.

V. The four living creatures and the four and twenty elders fell down before the Lamb.
R. Each held golden vessels full of incense, which are the prayers of the saints.

Let us pray. *(Silence)*

Almighty God, whose only-begotten Son received from the wise men a gift of incense and made for us the pure oblation foretold by the prophet: We dedicate to your worship *this vessel*, that our prayers may ascend in your sight as the incense, and the pure oblation of our Lord be proclaimed from farthest east to farthest west; through Jesus Christ our Lord. *Amen.*

19. Surplices and Albs

Antiphon

A great multitude which no one could number, from every nation and tribe and people and tongue, stand before the throne and before the Lamb.

V. He has clothed me with garments of salvation:
R. He has covered me with the robe of righteousness.

Let us pray. *(Silence)*

O God, before whose heavenly throne your servants minister to you, clothed in white robes: Accept *this* _____ which we dedicate for the use of the *ministers* of your Church, that serving before your earthly throne, they may worship you in spirit and in truth; through Jesus Christ our Lord. *Amen.*

20. Vestments for the Liturgy

Antiphon

You shall make holy garments for Aaron, for glory and for beauty.

V.   Clothe your ministers with righteousness:
R.   Let your people sing with joy.

Let us pray.   *(Silence)*

O God, you revealed your Son clothed in majesty and glory: Accept *this* _____ for the use of the *clergy* of your Church, that, being clothed with humility as they minister to you, they may show forth his eternal splendor; through Jesus Christ our Lord. *Amen.*

21. A Funeral Pall

Antiphon

I will greatly rejoice in the Lord; my soul shall exult in my God.

V.   He has clothed me with the garments of salvation;
R.   He has covered me with the robe of righteousness.

Let us pray. *(Silence)*

O God, who baptized us into the Body of your Son Jesus Christ, and made us members with different functions, all necessary and all to be honored: Make this pall a sign of our common membership in Christ, that we may know those who have departed this earthly life, not as the world esteems them, but as you know and love them; through Jesus Christ our Lord. *Amen.*

22. Any Church Ornament

Antiphon

Solomon beautified the sanctuary, and multiplied the vessels of the temple.

V. Oh, the majesty and magnificence of God's presence!
R. Oh, the power and the splendor of his sanctuary!

Let us pray. *(Silence)*

O God, whose blessed Son has sanctified and transfigured the use of material things: Receive *this* _____ which we offer, and grant that *it* may proclaim your love, benefit your Church, and minister grace and joy to those who use *it*; through Jesus Christ our Lord. *Amen.*

A Longer Form of Dedication

The longer form begins in the following manner.

The gift may be presented to the Celebrant with these words

I (We) present to you this _____ to be set apart for the service of Christ's holy Church.

The following versicles and prayer may be said

V. All things come from you, O Lord;
R. And from your own gifts do we give to you.
V. Prosper the work of our hands;
R. Prosper our handiwork.
V. Show your servants your works;
R. And your splendor to their children.

Let us pray.

Almighty God, we thank you that you have put it into the hearts of your people to make offerings for your service, and have been pleased to accept their gifts. Be with us now and bless us as we set apart *this* _____ to your praise and glory [and in memory (honor) of _____]; through Jesus Christ our Lord. *Amen.*

The proper form of dedication follows.

After the dedication, one or both of the following prayers may be said. Alternatively, the benefactors and persons to be commemorated may be remembered in the Prayers of the People.

In Commemoration

Almighty God, we remember before you today your faithful *servant N. (N.)*; and we pray that, having opened to *him* the gates of larger life, you will receive *him* more and more into your joyful service, that, with all who have faithfully served you in the past, *he* may share in the eternal victory of Jesus Christ our Lord. *Amen.*

For Benefactors

We bless your Name, O Lord, because it has pleased you to enable your *servant N. (N.)* to offer *this gift* for your worship. Remember *him* for good, and grant that all who benefit from *this gift* may show their thankfulness to you by using *it* in accordance with your will; through Jesus Christ our Lord. *Amen.*

The Founding of a Church

Ground Breaking

Before the service, four stakes are set in the ground, at the corners of the proposed building. Three cords are prepared, two to extend diagonally from corner to corner, a third to enclose the space. A spade is placed at the site of the Altar.

The bishop, or a priest appointed by the bishop, is the celebrant. Having vested nearby, the ministers, with the people, go in procession to the site of the building.

This Litany for the Church is sung or said during the procession.

God the Father, Creator of heaven and earth,
Have mercy on us.

God the Son, Redeemer of the world,
Have mercy on us.

God the Holy Spirit, Sanctifier of the faithful,
Have mercy on us.

Holy, blessed, and glorious Trinity, one God,
Have mercy on us.

O Christ the Rock, on which your people, as living stones joined together, grow into a spiritual house;
Defend your Church, we pray.

O Christ the Vine, of which your people are the branches;
Defend your Church, we pray.

O Christ the Head of the Body, of which your people are the members;
Defend your Church, we pray.

O Christ our Prophet, you teach the way of God in truth;
Defend your Church, we pray.

O Christ our Priest, you offered yourself upon the Cross, and now make intercession for us to the Father;
Defend your Church, we pray.

O Christ our King, you reign over all the earth, and make us citizens of your heavenly kingdom;
Defend your Church, we pray.

O Christ, you sent the Holy Spirit upon the Church, clothing it with power from on high;
Defend your Church, we pray.

We pray to you, Lord Christ.
Lord, hear our prayer.

That we may be devoted to the Apostles' teaching and fellowship, to the breaking of bread and the prayers,
Lord, hear our prayer.

That we may make disciples of all nations, baptizing them in the Name of the Father, and of the Son, and of the Holy Spirit,
Lord, hear our prayer.

That you will fulfill your promise to be with us always, even
to the ages of ages,
Lord, hear our prayer.

That you will sustain all members of your holy Church, that
in our vocation and ministry we may truly and devoutly
serve you,
Lord, hear our prayer.

That you will bless the clergy of your Church, that they may
diligently preach the Gospel and faithfully celebrate the holy
Sacraments,
Lord, hear our prayer.

That you will heal the divisions in your Church, that all may
be one, even as you and the Father are one,
Lord, hear our prayer.

Arise, O God, maintain your cause;
Do not forget the lives of the poor.

Look down from heaven, behold and tend this vine;
Preserve what your right hand has planted.

Let your priests be clothed with righteousness;
Let your faithful people sing with joy.

The Celebrant says

       The Lord be with you.
People   And also with you.
Celebrant Let us pray.

Let your continual mercy cleanse and defend your Church,
O Lord; and, because it cannot continue in safety without
your help, protect and govern it always by your goodness;
through Jesus Christ our Lord, who lives and reigns with
you and the Holy Spirit, one God, for ever and ever. *Amen.*

Glory to God whose power, working in us, can do infinitely more than we ask or imagine: Glory to him from generation to generation in the Church, and in Christ Jesus for ever and ever. *Amen.*

A hymn may be sung.

Then a Person appointed reads

Genesis 28:10-17

A sermon or address may follow.

While the following antiphon and psalm are being sung, persons appointed stretch two cords diagonally across the space, from the northeast to the southwest, and from the southeast to the northwest, securing them to the stakes, thus forming the Greek letter X (chi), the symbol both of the cross and of the name of Christ.

Antiphon   (*to be used before and after the Psalm*)

Let us go to God's dwelling place; let us fall upon our knees before his footstool.

Psalm 132:1-9 (10-19)

During the following antiphon and psalm, persons appointed stretch the third cord completely around the four stakes, enclosing the area. They move clockwise, beginning and ending at the southeast corner.

The ministers and people may follow in procession.

Antiphon

How wonderful is God in his holy places! the God of Israel, giving strength and power to his people! Blessed be God!

Psalm 48:1-3, 7-13

Then the Celebrant, standing at the site of the Altar, says

Since faithful people desire to build a house of prayer, dedicated to the glory of God [and in honor of _____] [to be known as _____], on this ground, now marked with the symbol of Christ;

Then, taking the spade, and breaking the ground, the Celebrant continues

Therefore, I break ground for this building, in the Name of the Father, and of the Son, and of the Holy Spirit.

May the Gospel be preached,
the Sacraments administered,
and prayers and praises offered
in this place, from generation to generation. *Amen.*

The Celebrant then says

         The Lord be with you.
People   And also with you.
Celebrant Let us pray.

People and Celebrant

Our Father, who art in heaven,
   hallowed be thy Name,
   thy kingdom come,
   thy will be done,
      on earth as it is in heaven.
Give us this day our daily bread.
And forgive us our trepasses,
   as we forgive those
      who trespass against us.
And lead us not into temptation,
   but deliver us from evil.
For thine is the kingdom,
   and the power, and the glory,
   for ever and ever. Amen.
	Our Father in heaven,
	   hallowed be your Name,
	   your kingdom come,
	   your will be done,
	      on earth as in heaven.
	Give us today our daily bread.
	Forgive us our sins
	   as we forgive those
	      who sin against us.
	Save us from the time of trial,
	   and deliver us from evil.
	For the kingdom, the power,
	   and the glory are yours,
	   now and for ever. Amen.

V. How wonderful is God in his holy places!
R. Establish, O God, what you have wrought for us.
V. Be favorable and gracious to Zion:
R. Build up the walls of Jerusalem.

Celebrant Let us pray.

O Lord God of Israel, the heavens cannot contain you, yet you are pleased to dwell in the midst of your people, and have moved us to set apart a space on which to build a house of prayer: Accept and bless the work which we have now begun, that it may be brought to completion, to the honor and glory of your holy Name; through Jesus Christ our Lord, who lives and reigns with you in the unity of the Holy Spirit, one God, for ever and ever. *Amen.*

A Deacon or the Celebrant then dismisses the people.

Laying of a Cornerstone

If the laying of a cornerstone takes place before the building is erected, the following order may be observed.

1. A hymn or anthem is sung.

2. A suitable passage of Scripture, such as Ephesians 2:19-22, may be read.

3. An address follows.

4. An appropriate prayer, such as the Collect of the Patron or Title of the Church, is said.

5. The cornerstone is then laid, after which the Celebrant prays as follows

Let us pray.

Lord Jesus Christ, Son of the living God, you are the brightness of the Father's glory and the express image of his person, the one foundation and the chief cornerstone: Bless what we have now done in the laying of this stone. Be the beginning, the increase, and the consummation of this work undertaken to the glory of your Name; who with the Father and the Holy Spirit live and reign, one God, for ever and ever. *Amen.*

Trumpets may be sounded, and the Celebrant says

Praise the Lord, because the foundation of the house of the Lord is laid!

The People respond, with a loud voice

Alleluia! Alleluia! Alleluia!

Applause may follow.

6. A hymn is sung, after which the rite is concluded with a blessing and dismissal.

If the laying of a cornerstone takes place after the building is completed, it is suitable that it take place in the context of a celebration of the Holy Eucharist. After the homily, a hymn, psalm, or anthem is sung, during which all go in procession to the site of the ceremony. An appropriate prayer (such as the Collect of the Patron or Title of the Church) is said, after which the cornerstone is laid. The rite then continues with the Celebrant's prayer given above. During the hymn that follows, the procession returns to the church where the Liturgy continues with (the Creed and) the Prayers of the People.

Restoring of Things Profaned

When a church building, altar, font, or other objects that have been set apart or consecrated, have been profaned, they may be restored to sacred use with the following form.

The bishop, or a priest, with such attendants as are appropriate, may go in procession around the exterior or interior of the church, or chapel, and then go to each object that has been profaned.

During the procession, Psalm 118 may be sung or said, with the following antiphon

I saw water proceeding out of the temple; from the right side it flowed, alleluia; and all those to whom that water came shall be saved, and shall say, alleluia, alleluia.

After the procession, each profaned object is addressed, and may be symbolically cleansed by the use of signs of purification, such as water or incense. The Celebrant touches or extends a hand toward each object and says

I declare this _____ restored to the use for which it has been dedicated and consecrated.

Then the Celebrant, standing in the midst of the church, says

Our help is in the Name of the Lord:
People   The maker of heaven and earth.

Celebrant The Lord be with you.
People   And also with you.

Celebrant Let us pray.   *(Silence)*

Almighty God, by the radiance of your Son's appearing you
have purified a world corrupted by sin: We humbly pray that
you would continue to be our strong defense against the
attacks of our enemies; and grant that [*this* _____,
and] whatsoever in this *church* has been stained or defiled
through the craft of Satan or by human malice, may be
purified and cleansed by your abiding grace; that this place,
purged from all pollution, may be restored and sanctified, to
the glory of your Name; through Jesus Christ our Lord, who
lives and reigns with you and the Holy Spirit, one God, now
and for ever. *Amen.*

Secularizing a Consecrated Building

The Altar(s) and all consecrated and dedicated objects that are to be preserved are removed from the building before the service begins.

The bishop, or a minister appointed by the bishop, presides.

The clergy of the congregation, the churchwardens, and other persons who desire to participate, assemble in the building.

The Presiding Minister, using these or similar words, says

We who are gathered here know that this building, which has been consecrated and set apart for the ministry of God's holy Word and Sacraments, will no longer be used in this way, but will be taken down (used for other purposes).

To many of you this building has been hallowed by cherished memories, and we know that some will suffer a sense of loss. We pray that they will be comforted by the knowledge that the presence of God is not tied to any place or building.

The *Altar has* been removed and protected from desecration.

It is the intention of the diocese that the congregation which worshiped here will not be deprived of the ministry of Word and Sacrament.

Let the [bishop's] Declaration of Secularization now be read.

Then a Warden, or other person appointed, reads the bishop's Declaration, which is to be in the following form

In the Name of the Father, and of the Son, and of the Holy Spirit. Amen.

On the _____ day of _____, in the year of our Lord _____, by *N.N.*, Bishop of _____, this building was duly dedicated and consecrated in honor of _____ [and named _____].

The Sentence of Consecration has been in effect until this present date.

I, *N.N.*, Bishop of _____, do hereby revoke the said Sentence [issued by my predecessor], and do remit this building, and all objects remaining in it, for any lawful and reputable use, according to the laws of this land.

This building, having now been declared deconsecrated and secularized, I declare to be no longer subject to my canonical jurisdiction.

This Declaration, which is to be publicly proclaimed before witnesses gathered at the said building, is given under my hand and seal, in the *City* of _____, *State* of _____, and Diocese of _____, on this _____ day of _____, in the year of our Lord _____.

    (signed) _____

    Bishop of _____

After the foregoing Declaration has been read, the Presiding Minister says

says	The Lord be with you.
People	And also with you.
Minister	Let us pray.

Minister and People

    Our Father . . . .

Then the Presiding Minister says

Lord God, in your great goodness you once accepted to your honor and glory this building, now secularized: Receive our praise and thanksgiving for the blessings, help, and comfort which you bestowed upon your people in this place. Continue, we pray, your many mercies in your Church, that we may be conscious at all times of your unchanging love; through Jesus Christ our Lord. *Amen.*

Assist us mercifully, O Lord, in these our prayers, and dispose the way of your servants towards the attainment of everlasting salvation; that among the swift and varied changes of this world, our hearts may surely there be fixed where true joys are to be found; through Jesus Christ our Lord. *Amen.*

The Lord bless us and keep us. *Amen.*
The Lord make his face to shine upon us,
    and be gracious to us. *Amen.*
The Lord lift up his countenance upon us,
    and give us peace. *Amen.*

The Peace may be exchanged.

Episcopal Services

Consecration of Chrism apart from Baptism

Provision is made in the rite of Holy Baptism for the consecration of Chrism in local congregations for use by a priest at baptisms in that church which take place on subsequent occasions in the year.

The following form is intended for use when, because of the absence of candidates for Baptism, the consecration of Chrism takes place at the time of Confirmation (see the last rubric on page 419 of the Prayer Book), or at some other time. The rite takes place immediately after the postcommunion prayer, and before the bishop's blessing and the dismissal.

The olive oil to be consecrated should be prepared in an ampulla or other vessel large enough to be seen clearly by the congregation. Traditionally, a small amount of oil of balsam or other fragrant oil is added to it, either before the service, or just before the consecratory prayer.

If desired, the vessel of oil may be brought forward in the offertory procession, received by a deacon or other minister, and then placed on a convenient side table until needed.

Immediately after the postcommunion prayer, the ampulla is brought to the bishop, who places it on a small table in the sight of the congregation, or on the altar (the communion vessels having already been removed).

Facing the people, the Bishop addresses them in these or similar words

Dear Friends in Christ: In the beginning, the Spirit of God hovered over the creation; and, throughout history, God, by the gift of the Holy Spirit, has empowered his people to serve him. As a sign of that gift, the priests and kings of Israel were anointed with oil; and our Lord Jesus was himself anointed with the Holy Spirit at his Baptism as the Christ, God's own Messiah. At Baptism, Christians are likewise anointed by that same Spirit to empower them for God's service. Let us now set apart this oil to be the sign of that anointing.

Let us pray.   *(Silence)*

The Bishop then places a hand on the vessel of oil and prays

Eternal Father, whose blessed Son was anointed by the Holy Spirit to be the Savior and servant of all, we pray you to consecrate this oil, that those who are sealed with it may share in the royal priesthood of Jesus Christ; who lives and reigns with you and the Holy Spirit, for ever and ever. *Amen.*

The Liturgy then concludes in the usual way with the Bishop's blessing and the dismissal.

A Proper for the Consecration of Chrism

If there is a need to consecrate Chrism at a separate, diocesan, service, the following Proper may be used:

Collect

Almighty God, who by the power of the Holy Spirit anointed your Son to be Messiah and Priest for ever, grant that all whom you have called to his service may confess the faith of Christ crucified, proclaim his resurrection, and share in his eternal priesthood; who lives and reigns with you in the unity of the same Spirit, one God, now and for ever. *Amen.*

Old Testament   Isaiah 61:1-8
Psalm   23,   *or*   89:20-29
Epistle   Revelation 1:4-8
Gospel   Luke 4:16-21

The Chrism is consecrated as described on page 209.

Reaffirmation
of Ordination Vows

This form is intended for use at a celebration of the Eucharist upon an occasion when the clergy are gathered together with the bishop.

It may also be used on the occasion of the reception of a priest from another Communion or of a restoration to the ministry.

If the Renewal of Ordination Vows takes place on Maundy Thursday, it should be done at a celebration of the Eucharist other than the Proper Liturgy of the day.

The following Collect may be used

Almighty God, giver of all good gifts, in your divine providence you have appointed various orders of ministers in your Church: Give your grace, we humbly pray, to all who are called to any office and ministry for your people; and so fill them with the truth of your doctrine, and clothe them with holiness of life, that they may faithfully serve before you, to the glory of your great Name and for the benefit of your holy Church; through Jesus Christ our Lord, who lives and reigns with you, in the unity of the Holy Spirit, one God, now and for ever. *Amen.*

The Psalm and Lessons may be those appointed for Ordination, or those for the Celebration of a New Ministry.

After the Sermon (and Creed), the Bishop sits in a chair before the Altar and addresses those who are to renew their vows. They stand facing the Bishop, who says these or similar words

Dear friends, the ministry we share is none other than the sacrificial ministry of Christ, who gave himself up to death on the cross for the salvation of the world. By his glorious resurrection he has opened for us the way of everlasting life. By the gift of the Holy Spirit he shares with us the riches of his grace.

We are called to proclaim his death and resurrection, to administer the Sacraments of the New Covenant which he sealed with his blood on the cross, and to care for his people in the power of the Spirit.

Do you here, in the presence of Christ and his Church, renew your commitment to your ministry, under the pastoral direction of your bishop?

Answer   I do.

Bishop   Do you reaffirm your promise to give yourself to prayer and study?

Answer   I do.

Bishop   Do you reaffirm your promise so to minister the Word of God and the Sacraments of the New Covenant that the reconciling love of Christ may be known and received?

Answer   I do.

Bishop   Do you reaffirm your promise to be a faithful servant of all those committed to your care, patterning your life in accordance with the teachings of Christ, so that you may be a wholesome example to your people?

Answer   I do.

The Bishop then stands and makes this affirmation

And now, as your bishop, I, too, before God and you, re-dedicate myself and reaffirm the promises that I made when I was ordained. I ask your prayers.

Bishop and Clergy

May the Lord who has given us the will to do these things, give us also the grace and power to perform them.

The Bishop then says

The peace of the Lord be always with you.
People   And also with you.

The Peace is then exchanged throughout the congregation.

The service continues with the Prayers of the People, or with the Offertory.

When this form is used for the reception of a priest from another Communion as a priest in this Church (the canonical requirements having been fulfilled), or for a restoration to the ministry, the service may be adapted as necessary, and the following question and answer are inserted immediately before the bishop's affirmation at the top of this page.

Will you be loyal to the doctrine, discipline, and worship of Christ as this Church has received them? And will you, in accordance with the canons of this Church, obey your bishop and other ministers who may have authority over you and your work?

Answer

I am willing and ready to do so; and I solemnly declare that I do believe the Holy Scriptures of the Old and New Testament to be the Word of God, and to contain all things necessary to salvation; and I do solemnly engage to conform to the doctrine, discipline, and worship of The Episcopal Church.

The newly received or restored priest is greeted personally by the bishop at the exchange of the Peace, and, having put on the vestments proper to the order, stands at the Altar with the bishop as a concelebrant at the Eucharist.

A newly restored deacon is greeted in the same way, and, properly vested, prepares the bread and wine at the Offertory.

Concerning the Service

This rite is designed for the recognition, investiture (and seating) of a bishop who has previously been ordained and consecrated in and for another diocese. It may be adapted to the circumstances of a former suffragan bishop who has been elected as diocesan bishop, or for a former bishop coadjutor who succeeds to the see.

The Presiding Bishop of the Church, or another bishop deputized for the occasion, presides at the rite.

The President of the Standing Committee of the Diocese serves as Warden.

Representative presbyters, deacons, and lay persons are assigned appropriate duties in the service.

The Readings and Psalm may be selected from the Proper of the Day, from those appointed for the Ordination of a Bishop, or from those appointed for Various Occasions.

The rubrics envisage the service taking place in the Cathedral Church. It may, however, be held in some other suitable place, and the service may be adapted when necessary.

One adaptation which will frequently need to be made is the omission of the seating of the bishop in the cathedra. In this case, immediately following the taking of the oath, the Presiding Bishop invites the people to greet their new bishop. The people offer their acclamations and applause, and the service continues with the exchange of the peace.

If a pastoral staff is used, it is carried by the former bishop in the welcoming procession, and presented to the new bishop at the time appointed. In the absence of the former bishop, it is placed on the Altar before the service begins.

The Bible to be used at the taking of the Oath is placed on the Altar before the beginning of the service.

If, for any reason, there is no Communion, the service concludes after the Peace with the singing of a hymn or anthem, the Lord's Prayer, the bishop's blessing, and the dismissal.

Recognition and Investiture of a Diocesan Bishop

The Recognition

When the ministers and people have assembled in the Cathedral Church, the principal doors having been closed, the Presiding Bishop is escorted from the sacristy to a chair placed at the entrance to the chancel, facing the people.

A welcoming procession is formed, and moves through the congregation to the principal door.

The new Bishop, attended by two deacons, standing outside the door, knocks upon it three times.

The Warden opens the door. As the door is opened, the Bishop's voice is heard, saying

Open for me the gates of righteousness; I will enter them and give thanks to the Lord.

Warden   The Lord prosper you;
we wish you well in the Name of the Lord.

A psalm or anthem is sung, during which the bishop is escorted by the welcoming procession to a place before the Presiding Bishop. Psalm 23 is appropriate, with the following antiphon

I will give you a shepherd after my own heart, who will feed you with knowledge and understanding.

The new Bishop petitions as follows

I, *N.N.,* whom God has ordained to be a shepherd and servant, and who now have been chosen as Bishop of this Diocese, come to you, desiring to be recognized, and invested, [and seated in the chair which is the symbol of that office].

The Presiding Bishop replies

Before I can accede to your petition, we must be assured by the appointed representative of the Diocese that you will be received as their duly elected Bishop.

The Warden then says

We are ready and willing to do so. As President of the Standing Committee, I certify that *N.N.* was duly elected Bishop of the Diocese of _____ by the clergy and people in Diocesan Convention assembled on the _____ day of _____, _____, and that consents to the election have been received from (a majority of the Bishops of the Church having jurisdiction and of the Standing Committees of the Dioceses) (the two houses of the General Convention). We therefore present to you the Right Reverend *N.N.* to be invested for the exercise of the office to which *he* has been chosen.

The Presiding Bishop then says

Let the will of the people here present be made known. Do you recognize and receive *N.* as your Bishop?

People   We do.

Presiding Bishop

Will you uphold N. in this ministry?

People   We will.

The Presiding Bishop stands and calls the people to prayer, in these or similar words

Let us now offer our prayers for N., for this Diocese, and for all God's people.

All kneel, and the Person appointed leads the Litany for Ordinations, or some other approved litany. At the end of the litany, after the Kyries (which may be sung by the congregation or choir in threefold, sixfold, or ninefold form), the Presiding Bishop stands and says

The Lord be with you.

People   And also with you.

Presiding Bishop.   Let us pray.

The Presiding Bishop then says the Collect of the Day or the Collect for Ordination.

All sit, and the Liturgy of the Word continues in the usual manner.

After the Sermon (and Creed), the following renewal of the commitments of ordination may take place.

The Presiding Bishop addresses the new Bishop in these or similar words

My *brother*, it has pleased God to call you to be the shepherd and chief pastor of this Diocese. I am sure that long before now you have laid to heart the high trust and weighty obligations of this office. But, in order that this congregation may know your commitment to fulfill this trust, I call upon you to reaffirm the promises you made when you were ordained and consecrated a bishop.

	Will you exercise your ministry in obedience to Christ?
Answer	I will obey Christ, and will serve in his name.

Presiding Bishop Will you be faithful in prayer, and in the study of Holy Scripture, that you may have the mind of Christ?

Answer I will, for he is my help.

Presiding Bishop Will you boldly proclaim and interpret the Gospel of Christ, enlightening the minds and stirring up the conscience of your people?

Answer I will, in the power of the Spirit.

Presiding Bishop As chief priest and pastor, will you encourage and support all baptized people in their gifts and ministries, nourish them from the riches of God's grace, pray for them without ceasing, and celebrate with them the sacraments of our redemption?

Answer I will, in the name of Christ, the Shepherd and Bishop of our souls.

Presiding Bishop Will you guard the faith, unity, and discipline of the Church?

Answer I will, for the love of God.

Presiding Bishop Will you share with your fellow bishops in the government of the whole Church; will you sustain your fellow presbyters and take counsel with them; will you guide and strengthen the deacons and all others who minister in the Church?

Answer I will, by the grace given me.

Presiding Bishop Will you be merciful to all, show compassion to the poor and strangers, and defend those who have no helper?

Answer I will, for the sake of Jesus Christ.

Presiding Bishop	May the Lord who has given you the will to do these things, give you the grace and power to perform them.
Answer	Amen.

The Investiture

The Presiding Bishop now stands and says

My *brother*, you have been recognized as a bishop of the Church and as bishop of this Diocese. Now I, *N.N.*, by the authority committed to me, and with the consent of those who have chosen you, do invest you, *N.N.*, as Bishop of _____ , with all the temporal and spiritual rights and responsibilities that pertain to that office; in the Name of the Father, and of the Son, and of the Holy Spirit. *Amen.*

If a pastoral staff is to be given, it is presented by the former Bishop of the Diocese, or it is brought from the Altar and presented by the Warden. The one who delivers the staff says

On behalf of the people and clergy of the Diocese of _____ , I give into your hands this pastoral staff. May Christ the good Shepherd uphold you and sustain you as you carry it in his name. *Amen.*

A Bible is brought from the Altar and held before the Bishop, who, laying a hand upon it, takes the oath, as follows

I, *N.N.*, Bishop in the Church of God, now duly invested and acknowledged as Bishop of this Diocese [receive this pastoral staff at your hands as a token of my jurisdiction and of your recognition, and] do solemnly promise that I will observe, and to the utmost of my power fulfill, the responsibilities and obligations of this office, striving in all things to be a faithful shepherd to the flock of Christ. So help me God. *Amen.*

The Seating

The Presiding Bishop and the Warden now escort the bishop to the chair designated for the Bishop of the Diocese. Meanwhile, instrumental music may be played.

The Dean of the Cathedral Church, meeting the Bishop at the Cathedra, says

In the name of *the Chapter* of this Cathedral Church, and on behalf of the people of this Diocese, I install you, N., in the chair appointed to your office. May the Lord stir up in you the flame of holy charity, and the power of faith that overcomes the world. *Amen.*

The Bishop sits, and the People offer their acclamations and applause.

Bells may be rung and trumpets sounded.

Afterwards, the Bishop stands and says

      The peace of the Lord be always with you.
People   And also with you.

The Presiding Bishop and other Ministers greet the Bishop.

The People greet one another.

The Bishop greets other members of the clergy, family members, and members of the congregation as may be convenient.

The Liturgy continues with the Offertory.

Deacons prepare the Table.

The Bishop goes to the Lord's Table as chief Celebrant and, joined by other bishops and representative presbyters of the diocese, proceeds with the celebration of the Eucharist.

In place of the usual postcommunion prayer, a Bishop or Presbyter leads the people in the following

Almighty Father, we thank you for feeding us with the holy food of the Body and Blood of your Son, and for uniting us through him in the fellowship of your Holy Spirit. We thank you for raising up among us faithful servants for the ministry of your Word and Sacraments. We pray that N. may be to us an effective example in word and action, in love and patience, and in holiness of life. Grant that we, with *him*, may serve you now, and always rejoice in your glory; through Jesus Christ your Son our Lord, who lives and reigns with you and the Holy Spirit, one God, now and for ever. Amen.

The new Bishop blesses the people, first saying

	Our help is in the name of the Lord;
People	The maker of heaven and earth.
Bishop	Blessed be the name of the Lord;
People	From this time forth for evermore.
Bishop	The blessing, mercy, and grace of God Almighty, the Father, the Son, and the Holy Spirit, be upon you, and remain with you for ever. *Amen.*

A Deacon dismisses the People.

Concerning the Service

This service is intended for use when a new bishop has not been seated in the cathedra of the diocese at the time of ordination or at the time of recognition and investiture.

Normally, it will take place on the occasion of the first visit of the bishop to the Cathedral.

On a Sunday or other major Holy Day the Proper is that of the Day. On other days it may be one of those appointed for Various Occasions.

If, however, the seating takes place shortly after the service of ordination or investure held on the same day in a place other than the Cathedral, only the opening ceremonies of this service are used, concluding after the Te Deum or Gloria in excelsis with the Lord's Prayer, the bishop's blessing, and the dismissal.

Welcoming and Seating
of a Bishop in the Cathedral

The ministers and people assemble in the Cathedral Church.

The principal door being closed, the Dean, the Cathedral clergy (the Cathedral Chapter), and other representative persons as convenient, go in procession through the congregation to the principal door. The people stand.

The new bishop, attended by two deacons, standing outside, knocks three times on the door.

The Warden opens the door, and the Bishop enters and greets the congregation, saying

Grace and peace be with you, from God our Father and the Lord Jesus Christ.

People   And also with you.

A psalm or anthem is sung, during which the Bishop is escorted by the welcoming procession to a place in full sight of the people.

The Dean, or other person appointed, welcomes the bishop in these or similar words

N.N., Bishop in the Church of God, and our Bishop, we welcome you to your Cathedral Church, the symbol and center of your pastoral, liturgical, and teaching ministry in this Diocese.

The Bishop responds, saying

I, *N.N.*, your Bishop, thank you for your welcome. I promise, God helping me, to be a faithful shepherd and servant among you. I pray that the ministry which we will share may be pleasing to God, and that it may strengthen the life of this diocese, and the whole Church of God. I now ask to be seated in the chair that is the symbol of my office.

The bishop is escorted to the Cathedra. Meanwhile, instrumental music may be played.

The Dean, standing near the Cathedra, says

In the name of *the Chapter* of this Cathedral Church, and on behalf of the people of this diocese, I install you, *N.*, in the chair appointed to your office. May the Lord stir up in you the flame of holy charity, and the power of faith that overcomes the world. *Amen.*

The Bishop sits, and the People offer their acclamations and applause.

Bells may be rung and trumpets sounded.

The Bishop stands, and the Te Deum, the Gloria in excelsis, or other song of praise is sung.

The Bishop then says to the people

	The Lord be with you.
People	And also with you.
Bishop	Let us pray.

The Bishop says the Collect of the Day.

The Liturgy continues in the usual way, with the appointed Lessons and Psalm.

At the Great Thanksgiving, the Bishop, as the principal Celebrant, is joined at the Altar by the presbyters of the Cathedral, and other priests as desired.

In place of the usual postcommunion prayer, the Dean leads the people in the following

Almighty Father, we thank you for feeding us with the holy food of the Body and Blood of your Son, and for uniting us through him in the fellowship of your Holy Spirit. We thank you for raising up among us faithful servants for the ministry of your Word and Sacraments. We pray that N. may be to us an effective example in word and action, in love and patience, and in holiness of life. Grant that we, with *him* may serve you now, and always rejoice in your glory; through Jesus Christ your Son our Lord, who lives and reigns with you and the Holy Spirit, one God, now and for ever. Amen.

The Bishop blesses the people, first saying

	Our help is in the Name of the Lord.
People	The maker of heaven and earth.
Bishop	Blessed be the Name of the Lord.
People	From this time forth for evermore.
Bishop	The blessing, mercy, and grace of God Almighty, the Father, the Son, and the Holy Spirit, be upon you and remain with you for ever. *Amen*.

A Deacon dismisses the people.

Setting Apart
for a Special Vocation

Individual Christians, in response to God's call, may wish to commit themselves to the religious life under vows made directly to the bishop of the diocese.

The order which follows is not intended to supplant forms in use for admitting members to religious communities.

Where life profession is intended, the process normally involves three stages: novitiate, temporary or annual vows, and life profession. In some instances, persons may choose not to proceed beyond the stage of annual vows.

The novitiate is a period of testing. Admission to the novitiate normally takes place at a weekday Daily Office, at the time of the hymn or anthem which follows the Collects. It involves a promise to accept and follow a specific and agreed-upon rule of life for a period of time prescribed by the bishop.

Temporary or annual vows are made at the satisfactory conclusion of the prescribed period of testing. At this time, the person takes vows of poverty, chastity, and obedience to the bishop, for a prescribed length of time. This stage involves the acceptance of the obligation to recite an approved form of the Daily Office. The rite takes place at a celebration of the Holy Eucharist, immediately after the Prayers of the People and before the Peace. Appropriate clothing may be presented as a sign of dedication.

Final or life vows are made at a festal celebration of the Holy Eucharist. At this time additional symbols of dedication may be given.

The order of the rite is identical for all three stages.

1. A request by the person to be admitted to the appropriate stage.

2. A sermon or homily, or an address to the person.

3. An examination by the bishop concerning the nature of the commitment and of the person's desire for this special vocation.

4. The promises or vows appropriate to the stage of profession.

5. The appropriate prayer or blessing appended to this order, or some other similar form.

6. The presentation of clothing and other symbols of special vocation.

Appropriate Lessons and Psalms

Old Testament

Genesis 12:1-4a (4b-8) (The Call of Abraham)
1 Samuel 3:1-11 (The Call of Samuel)
1 Kings 19:16b, 19-21 (The Call of Elisha)

Psalms

23 (The Lord is my shepherd)
24:1-6 (7-10) (Who can ascend the hill of the Lord?)
27:1-11 (12-18) (Your face, Lord, will I seek)
33:(1-11) 12-22 (The eye of the Lord is upon those who fear him)
34:1-8 (9-22) (I will bless the Lord at all times)
40:1-12 (I love to do your will, O my God)
63:1-12 (You are my God; eagerly I seek you)
100 (Serve the Lord with gladness)

New Testament

Acts 2:42-47 (The apostles' teaching and fellowship)
Acts 4:32-35 (They had everything in common)

1 Corinthians 1:22-31 (God chose what was foolish)
Philippians 3:8-14 (That I may gain Christ)
Colossians 3:12-17 (Put on love, which binds everything together)
1 John 4:7-16 (He who abides in love abides in God)

The Gospel

Matthew 16:24-27 (Let him take up his cross and follow me)
Matthew 19:3-12 (Eunuchs for the sake of the kingdom)
Matthew 19:16-26 (Sell what you possess and give to the poor)
John 15:1-8 (I am the vine, you are the branches)

Prayer for a Novice

Look with favor, Almighty God, upon this your servant N.,
who, in response to the prompting of the Holy Spirit, desires
to commit *himself* to you in a life of special vocation, and is
undertaking to embrace the three-fold path of poverty,
chastity, and obedience. Grant *him* the strength of your
grace to persevere in *his* endeavor, and the guidance of the
Spirit to find *his* true vocation. If it be your will that *he*
continue in this way, reveal this to *him*, we pray, and bring
him in due time to the taking of solemn vows; through Jesus
Christ our Lord, who lives and reigns with you and the Holy
Spirit, one God, for ever and ever. *Amen.*

Dedication of a Person Taking Temporary or Annual Vows

May God the Lord, who called Abraham to leave home and
kindred to journey to an unknown destination, and who led
the people of Israel by the hand of Moses his servant
through the desert to the promised land: Shepherd you in
your pilgrimage, and lead you by safe pathways, for his
Name's sake. *Amen.*

May God the Son, who, in his earthly life, was often solitary but never alone, because the Father was with him: Be your constant companion in your withdrawals from the busyness of the world, and support and strengthen you when you return refreshed to bear witness to the love and power of God. *Amen.*

May God the Holy Spirit, who helps us in our weakness, and intercedes for the saints in accordance with the Father's will: Teach you to pray as you ought to pray; strengthen you in purity of faith, in holiness of life, and in perfectness of love; and bind you ever more and more closely to the Father through the Son. *Amen.*

And may Almighty God, the holy and undivided Trinity, Father, Son, and Holy Spirit, guard your body, save your soul, and bring you safely to the heavenly country; where he lives and reigns for ever and ever. *Amen.*

Dedication of a Person Taking Life Vows

Blessed are you, O Lord our God, for your great love in sending into the world your only-begotten Son, who for us and for our salvation, emptied himself of his divine estate, and embraced a life apart from the consolations of family, having not even a place to lay his head. We bless your Name, also, that in every age and land you have called men and women to imitate their Lord, by setting zeal for your kingdom and its righteousness ahead of all worldly considerations, the love of your little ones above the claims of flesh and blood, and obedience to your will in place of all personal ambitions.

Accept, we pray, the life profession of this your servant *N.*, who, following the example of the Lord Jesus, of Anna the prophetess and holy Simeon, of the Lady Julian and Nicholas Ferrar [of _____], and of countless others of your saints, now offers *himself* for your service in a life of poverty, chastity, and obedience. Bestow upon *him* your Holy Spirit to dwell in *him* richly, to give *him* steadfastness of purpose, to sanctify *him* more and more fully, and to guide *him* surely into paths of service and of witness, to the honor and glory of your great Name; through Jesus Christ our Lord, who with you and the Holy Spirit lives and reigns, one God, now and for ever. *Amen.*

Appendix

Concerning the Service

This order is provided for use when a priest in charge of a congregation terminates a pastoral relationship. In other circumstances, appropriate actions of this rite may be used, and necessary alterations may be made.

It is the prerogative of the bishop to be present and to act as chief minister, or to appoint a deputy. However, the congregation and the departing minister may take leave of each other without the presence of the bishop or the bishop's representative. It is suggested that this service take place within a Eucharist, which begins in the usual way.

A Service for the Ending of a Pastoral Relationship and Leave-taking from a Congregation

At the Service of the Word

A hymn, psalm, or anthem may be sung.

The people standing, the Celebrant says,

Blessed be God: Father, Son, and Holy Spirit.

People   And blessed be his kingdom, now and forever.
Amen.

In place of the above, for Easter Day through the Day of Pentecost

Celebrant   Alleluia. Christ is risen.
People   The Lord is risen indeed. Alleluia.

In Lent and on other penitential occasions

Celebrant   Bless the Lord who forgives all our sins;
People   His mercy endures for ever.

The Celebrant then continues

          There is one Body and one Spirit;
People   There is one hope in God's call to us;
Celebrant   One Lord, one Faith, one Baptism;
People   One God and Father of all.

Celebrant The Lord be with you.
People   And also with you.
Celebrant Let us pray.

The Collect of the Day

At the principal service on a Sunday or other feast, the collect and lessons are properly those of the day. At other times, one of the following collects may be used.

Almighty and everlasting God, by whose Spirit the whole body of your faithful people is governed and sanctified: Receive our supplications and prayers, which we offer before you for all members of your holy Church, that in their vocation and ministry they may truly and devoutly serve you; through our Lord and Savior Jesus Christ, who lives and reigns with you and the Holy Spirit, one God, now and for ever. *Amen.*

O God of unchangeable power and eternal light: Look favorably on your whole Church, that wonderful and sacred mystery; by the effectual working of your providence, carry out in tranquility the plan of salvation; let the whole world see and know that things which were cast down are being raised up, and things which had grown old are being made new, and that all things are being brought to their perfection by him through whom all things were made, your Son Jesus Christ our Lord; who lives and reigns with you, in the unity of the Holy Spirit, one God, for ever and ever. *Amen.*

Direct us, O Lord, in all our doings with *thy* most gracious favor, and further us with *thy* continual help; that in all our works begun, continued, and ended in *thee,* we may glorify *thy* holy Name, and finally, by *thy* mercy, obtain everlasting life; through Jesus Christ our Lord. *Amen.*

Gracious Father, we pray for thy holy Catholic Church. Fill it with all truth, in all truth with all peace. Where it is corrupt, purify it; where it is in error, direct it; where in any thing it is amiss, reform it. Where it is right, strengthen it; where it is in want, provide for it; where it is divided, reunite it; for the sake of Jesus Christ thy Son our Savior. *Amen.*

Almighty Father, whose blessed Son before his passion prayed for his disciples that they might be one, as you and he are one: Grant that your Church, being bound together in love and obedience to you, may be united in one body by the one Spirit, that the world may believe in him whom you have sent, your Son Jesus Christ our Lord; who lives and reigns with you, in the unity of the Holy Spirit, one God, now and for ever. *Amen.*

or this collect

Lord, you have apportioned to your people the manifold gifts of the Spirit: Grant amid the changes of the world that your Church may abide, and be strengthened in ministry through continuous outpouring of your gifts; through Jesus Christ our Lord, who lives and reigns with you and the Holy Spirit, one God, for ever and ever. *Amen.*

The Ministry of the Word

Old Testament

Genesis 31:44-46, 48-49, 50b (The Lord watch between you and me when we are absent one from another.)

Genesis 12:1-9 (Abraham's departure from Haran and God's promise to bless him.)

Deuteronomy 18:15-18 (God will raise up a prophet like Moses.)

Deuteronomy 32:1-9 (The farewell of Moses.)

Joshua 24:1, 14-25 (Joshua's farewell to his people.)

Ecclesiastes 3:1-7; 7:8, 10, 13-14 (A time for everything; better the end than the beginning.)

Sirach 50:1, 11-24 (The service of the faithful priest.)

Psalm 119:89-96, or Nunc Dimittis

Epistle

1 Corinthians 3:4-11 (Paul planted, Apollos watered, God gave growth.)
Acts 16:9-10 (Paul's call from Macedonia.)
Acts 20:17-22, 25-28, 32, 36-38b (Paul's apologia for his ministry at
  Ephesus.)
II Thessalonians 2:13—3:5 (Paul gives thanks for the success of the
  Gospel.)
I Thessalonians 5:12-25 (Paul encourages the ministry among the
  Thessalonians.)
Philippians 4:1-10, 23 (Rejoice in the Lord always.)

Alleluia Verse: Alleluia. "I will instruct you in the way that you should
go; I will guide you with my eye says the Lord." Alleluia. (Psalm 32:9 or
Psalm 25:9) Tract; Psalm 18:33-37; Psalm 43:3-6; Psalm 78:1-8; Psalm
133.

Gospel

Matthew 9:35-38 (The harvest is plentiful, but the laborers are few.)
Matthew 25:31-40 (As you did it to the least of these, you did it to me.)
Luke 12:35-38 (The faithful servant.)
Luke 17:7-10 (We are unworthy servants; we have only done our duty.)
John 10:14-18 (The ministry of the good shepherd.)
John 21:15-19 (Feed my sheep.)

Sermon

*It maybe appropriate for the Bishop or the Bishop's Deputy to preach the
sermon, in the course of which a charge should be given to the
congregation regarding the nature of ministry.*

The service continues with the Nicene Creed.

The Ending of a Pastoral Relationship

Just before the Peace, the Minister addresses the Bishop (or the Bishop's Deputy) and the congregation with these or similar words

On the ____9TH____ day of ___November___, 19__86__, I was inducted by Bishop N. as rector of _____. I have, with God's help and to the best of my abilities, exercised this trust, accepting its privileges and responsibilities.

After prayer and careful consideration, it now seems to me that I should leave this charge, and I publicly state that my tenure as rector of _____ ends this day.

(The Minister may, if desired, briefly state his plans for the future.)

The Bishop or the Deputy says

Do you, the people of _____, recognize and accept the conclusion of this pastoral relationship?

People   We do.

If the Bishop or Bishop's Deputy is not present, the Minister may address a similar question to the congregation.

Then the Minister may express thanksgiving for the time of the tenure, with its joys and sorrows, and state hopes for the future of the congregation.

The Minister may present to the warden(s) a letter of resignation, the keys of the parish, the parish altar service book, the parish register, or other symbols fitting to the occasion.

The Minister may also express his thanks to the representatives of parish organizations and offices, and indicate that those organizations will continue to function.

The Minister may then be joined by members of his family, who may express what life with the congregation has meant to them. One or more representatives of the congregation may briefly respond to the Minister and family, and bid them godspeed. If it is appropriate, representatives of diocesan and community organizations in which the Minister or members of his family have been active may also speak.

The Bishop or the Bishop's Deputy may then indicate what provision has been made for the continuation of the ministries of the parish. He may declare the name of the locum tenens, *senior warden, or other person who is to have ecclesiastical responsibility, and may request, if it seems appropriate, other leaders in the parish to continue their leadership until a new incumbent is installed. He may express his feelings about the ministry now coming to its end.*

The departing Minister and the congregation then say together the following prayer

O God, you have bound us together for a time as priest and people to work for the advancement of your kingdom in this place: We give you humble and hearty thanks for the ministry which we have shared in these years now past.

Silence

We thank you for your patience with us despite our blindness and slowness of heart. We thank you for your forgiveness and mercy in the face of our many failures.

Silence

Especially we thank you for your never-failing presence with us through these years, and for the deeper knowledge of you and of each other which we have attained.

Silence

We thank you for those who have been joined to this part of Christ's family through baptism. We thank you for opening our hearts and minds again and again to your Word, and for feeding us abundantly with the Sacrament of the Body and Blood of your Son.

Silence

Now, we pray, be with those who leave and with us who stay; and grant that all of us, by drawing ever nearer to you, may always be close to each other in the communion of your saints. All this we ask for the sake of Jesus Christ, your Son, our Lord. *Amen.*

The departing Minister, or the Bishop, or the Bishop's Deputy then says

The peace of the Lord be always with you
People   And also with you.

If the Eucharist is to follow, the service continues with the offertory.

Except on major feasts, the Preface may be that for Apostles and Ordinations.

After the Communion

Almighty God, we thank you for feeding us with the holy food of the Body and Blood of your Son, and for uniting us through him in the fellowship of your Holy Spirit. We thank you for raising up among us faithful servants of your Wood and Sacraments. We thank you especially for the work of N. among us, *and the presence of* his *family here.* Grant that both *he* and we may serve you in the days ahead, and always rejoice in your glory, and come at length into your heavenly kingdom; through Jesus Christ our Lord. *Amen.*

This blessing may be pronounced either by the minister, or by the bishop, or by the Bishop's Deputy.

May God, who has led us in the paths of justice and truth, lead us still, and keep us in his ways. *Amen.*

May God, whose Son has loved us and given himself for us, love us still, and establish us in peace. *Amen.*

May God, whose Spirit unites us and fills our hearts with joy, illumine us still, and strengthen us for the years to come. *Amen.*

And the blessing of God Almighty, the Father, the Son, and the Holy Spirit, be upon you and remain with you for ever. *Amen.*

If the departing Minister is the Celebrant, one of the post-communion prayers from the Book of Common Prayer, *Holy Eucharist, Rite Two, pages 365-366, will be more appropriate.*